CONFEREN(
ON FUTURE STRU
OF POST-SECONDARY
PARIS 26th-29th JUNE 1973

GENERAL REPORT

POLICIES FOR HIGHER EDUCATION

ORGANISATION FOR ECONOMIC CO-OPERATION AND DEVELOPMENT   PARIS 1974

The Organisation for Economic Co-operation and Development (OECD) was set up under a Convention signed in Paris on 14th December, 1960, which provides that the OECD shall promote policies designed :

— *to achieve the highest sustainable economic growth and employment and a rising standard of living in Member countries, while maintaining financial stability, and thus to contribute to the development of the world economy;*
— *to contribute to sound economic expansion in Member as well as non-member countries in the process of economic development;*
— *to contribute to the expansion of world trade on a multilateral, non-discriminatory basis in accordance with international obligations.*

The Members of OECD are Australia, Austria, Belgium, Canada, Denmark, Finland, France, the Federal Republic of Germany, Greece, Iceland, Ireland, Italy, Japan, Luxembourg, the Netherlands, New Zealand, Norway, Portugal, Spain, Sweden, Switzerland, Turkey, the United Kingdom and the United States.

*
* *

The opinions expressed and arguments employed in this publication
are the responsibility of the authors

FOREWORD

Policies for higher education are under active consideration in most OECD countries. A major issue in such policies in the seventies will be the setting up of structures adapted to a stage of development which has either been or is at the point of being reached in most Member countries, that of the transition to mass higher education.

To discuss a number of major issues related to policies for the future development of higher education systems, the OECD organised, in the framework of the programme of work of its Education Committee, a Conference on Future Structures of Post-Secondary Education, which took place in Paris, June 1973. High officials responsible for education policy in OECD Member countries, including a number of ministers, attended the Conference together with teachers, administrators and participants from trade union and professional organisations.

The central concern of the Conference was to examine the advent of mass higher education in its main patterns and characteristics and to identify alternative policy measures for facilitating the overall structural transformation of the system towards meeting its new objectives in the context of social and economic development.

The present publication is the General Report of the Conference published under the title "Policies for Higher Education". A series of supporting studies which were prepared for the Conference will be grouped together in two companion volumes to be published by OECD: <u>Structure of Studies and Place of Research in Mass Higher Education</u> and <u>Towards Mass Higher Education: Trends, Issues and Dilemmas</u>.

CONTENTS

Part One

GENERAL PRESENTATION OF THE ISSUES

I

OPENING ADDRESS

by

Emile van Lennep

Secretary-General of the OECD

It gives me great pleasure to welcome such a distinguished audience of senior policy makers and experts from the Member countries to this OECD Conference on Future Structures of Post-Secondary Education.

Just over three years ago, I had the privilege of addressing in this same room a similar gathering to our Conference on Policies for Educational Growth. I said then that as Secretary-General of the OECD I was convinced of the importance of the relationship between education and economic and social development and of the role which the Organisation would continue to play in assisting Member governments in the discussion and formulation of policies in this area. Events in the intervening period, both within and outside the Organisation, have, if anything, reinforced this conviction, while the work which has led up to the present Conference is but one example of how the OECD has been able to evolve its role in response to the changing context of policy concerns in the Member countries.

Behind this changing context lies the general recognition, reiterated by the Ministerial Council of the Organisation earlier this month, that continued attention should be paid to the qualitative aspects of economic growth, that is to the acceptability of the end uses to which our productive resources and their increase are put, in order to ensure that policies are formulated which give fuller consideration to the various aspects of social well-being. Thus, one central issue in the 1970s for all our Member countries will be the definition and promotion of new social objectives, which will become increasingly important with the continuing rise in national and personal incomes. The Organisation itself is actively engaged in this process and the Council has recently approved a set of major social concerns for the OECD Member countries.

But the stronger emphasis on the distribution of output and of economic growth over different end uses and the continuous rise in new social demands leads to other central issues which will confront most of our Member countries over the present decade. It has always been true that the sum total of our private and social demands surpassed available resources, and therefore could not all be satisfied at the same time. The rise of new social demands in fields like education, the environment, health, social security and assistance forces us to give more thought to the problem of how best to reconcile these competing social demands with the limited resources available. Within the Organisation this problem has recently become the major concern of Working Party No. 2 of the Economic Policy Committee.

If policies for the allocation of resources are to reflect effectively the political will for the pursuit of the new social and economic objectives of the 1970s, it is necessary to establish closer co-ordination of policies between the various sectors and levels of public activity. This is a complicated matter, calling for a careful assessment of the effectiveness of the existing procedures and structures of government and of their reform. Within the Organisation we are now endeavouring to formulate the problems involved, so as to provide a basis on which our Member governments could begin to discuss possible approaches and solutions to what I would call the "horizontalization" of public policies.

I have dwelt on these broad issues because I believe that the area of post-secondary education is a perfect example of a field where policy formulation, institutional and substantive change and management have to be increasingly governed by the considerations cited, as is amply shown in the Secretariat analyses laid before you.

The educational system has indeed been one of the most rapidly growing sectors of society. In the period 1960-70, public education expenditure in OECD countries rose on average by 15% a year in current prices. The fastest rise was in higher education with a growth rate of 20% a year. This compares with a growth rate of total public expenditure of 12% a year. Public expenditure on education amounted on average to 5% of GNP in Member countries in 1970, but this is only part of the total cost, for over 60 million students in the system were of an age when they could have been working and their earnings foregone plus expenditure on on-the-job training were probably equal to more than the 5% of GNP represented by public educational spending.

With the new needs for recurrent education and/or diversification which are making themselves felt today, as set out in the reports before this Conference, there is every reason to expect that this rapid growth of post-secondary education will continue.

As resources are scarce and other pressing needs in the social field manifest themselves - such as those related to pollution, to the availability of our natural environment for recreational pursuits, to effect rapid and comfortable transportation between home and work and to care for the poor, sick, disabled and aged - it is particularly incumbent on those responsible to develop effective programmes which meet the real needs of society and make the best use of resources.

The post-secondary education system illustrates well these increasingly complex problems of management and co-ordination. It is linked on the one hand to the sources of the cultural and scientific sustenance of our societies; at the same time, it represents a main avenue of opportunities towards which individuals aspire for their personal and professional development and through which social equity and social mobility can be developed. In the present changed context it will be by no means easy to reconcile these twin attributes of the higher education system which may be broadly characterized as societal and individual respectively. Following the generalization of secondary education, we have experienced a massive rise in the demand for higher education which makes it difficult to reconcile the societal and individual objectives of the system. The new quest for widening the societal dimension of the post-secondary education system by taking up new responsibilities for the structure of society and the demand for enlarged autonomy and participation in such matters adds to this problem. Being by nature labour intensive, relative costs per unit are rising very fast and at the same time the increasing competing claims from various other sectors for public resources set limits to the possibilities of expansion.

On the other hand, rapid changes in the employment structure and in social attitudes may frustrate individual aspirations of students and need to be taken into account. Structural and pedagogical changes in the educational system are an essential but not a sufficient condition for a solution of these problems and governments of most Member countries are seeing important new responsibilities devolving on them in a new partnership with the academic community, accepting its essential autonomy, for the effective management of growth of and change in the system, in the context of their broader social and economic policies.

There is a growing awareness of this, as the list of subjects to be discussed during your Conference amply shows. I have been particularly struck by the extent to which current trends in the Member countries for the reorganisation of post-secondary education reflect a growing reaction to the continued growth of higher education in its present form - a feeling which seems to be shared by a wide range of opinion, from officials in administrations and planning offices to the general public and the students themselves. At the heart of this reaction lie the difficulties experienced in all Member countries in establishing satisfactory relationships between the offerings of the higher education system, the aspirations of its new clients and the needs and absorptive capacity of society for qualified people. This failure of adaptation, often quite unjustly attributed solely to the education system, is thus a complex educational, social and economic phenomenon which calls for deeper study of the interactions between the educational system and the employment situation, including working conditions, and a re-examination of educational policy in its relationships with other policies.

Any approach to such problems will of course require close consultation with the various social groups involved, particularly industry and the trade unions, and I am happy to see that these two sides, through their consultative bodies to the OECD, are represented at this Conference and will put forward the viewpoints of their respective organisations on the issues before us.

Future developments, I believe, will be significantly influenced not so much by a slackening in the social demand for higher education as by the need for more diversified facilities, in terms of spread-out time, physical location and programmes for adults as well as young people. With regard to the young, the crucial issue will be to develop a wider range of real options at the end of compulsory or secondary schooling, including possibilities for those who would prefer to enter active life to do so with the possibility of subsequent return to education at various levels. For both youth and adults, more flexible relationships between education and work experience are needed so that learning opportunities and career development become more interrelated over the whole life-span of the individual.

The resulting approach to policy - giving increasing importance to what more or less inter-changeably has been called "recurrent", "lifelong", "permanent" or "continuing" education and training - has been developed in various respects by the OECD Centre for Educational Research and Innovation, as well as by the OECD Committees for Education and for Manpower and Social Affairs. Application of this concept would bring together formal and informal youth and adult education programmes. It would thereby remove the finality of selection which operates in the present system. It would diminish the segregation of the working and the learning youth and forge stronger links between the education and training institutions, the economy and society. In the context of the growing importance of the social objectives in the end use of economic output and the orientation of economic growth which I have referred to earlier, the facilities provided by such a system become an indispensable condition of economic development itself.

A clarification of the issues involved in the policies which I have mentioned, in the broader context indicated, will be the essence of your deliberations during the next three days and I feel sure that the results of this Conference will be of great help to all those in our Member countries concerned with seeking practical and acceptable solutions to these problems. There can be no doubt that higher education is experiencing the winds of change. And I know that the conclusions you reach will help to guide future policies in this vital aspect of social development and I wish you success in this task.

II

OVERALL ISSUES IN THE DEVELOPMENT OF FUTURE STRUCTURES OF POST-SECONDARY EDUCATION

by

Ladislav Cerych, Dorotea Furth
and George S. Papadopoulos,
OECD Secretariat

CONTENTS

INTRODUCTION

1. SCOPE AND PURPOSE OF THE PAPER

A feeling of mounting uncertainty about the future development of higher education persists in most OECD countries. At the heart of it lie the strains created by the massive growth of individual demand for higher education, the inability of the system to adapt and make itself relevant to this largely autonomous demand, and the all-round failure to establish satisfactory relationships between the higher education system, the aspirations of students, and the needs and absorptive capacity of society for qualified people. There is, in consequence, a manifest urgency in the drive within Member countries towards structural reform of the entire post-secondary sector.

The central issue before this Conference is thus the transition from elitist to mass higher education which is now under way in the great majority of Member countries. This situation has been summed up as follows in an earlier Secretariat report:

> "Most countries are at an intermediary and critical stage, between elitist and mass higher education, the former having to be abandoned under the pressure of numbers and of a series of socio-economic factors, the latter requiring structures, content and organisational arrangements which have not yet been developed and only partly identified." (1)

Strategic aspects of the policy problems posed by this transition are dealt with in the series of background reports and studies which has been prepared on the specific themes of the Conference. The present paper endeavours to provide a general framework for the discussions by focussing on the implications of this situation from the point of view of the overall structures of the system. In providing the general context within which the essential interrelationships of all the items on the Conference agenda can be illustrated, this perspective should facilitate a global approach to the consideration of policy measures which are now in the centre of the public debate in all Member countries. The lag between quantitative expansion (and even existing access conditions) on the one hand, and adequate structures to accommodate the increased enrolments and the new student population on the other, seems in fact to be the most dramatic feature of the present situation, paralyzing progress towards new goals, particularly in the European Member countries.

In the discussion which follows two preliminary points should be kept in mind. First, the term "structures" in itself is neutral and value-

---

1.   "Towards New Structures of Post-Secondary Education: A Preliminary Statement of Issues", OECD Document, Paris, 1971, p. 28.

free: any system, traditional or revolutionary, conservative or progressive, implies a structure. "Structural reform", therefore, must be understood in the sense of a "policy instrument" for the implementation of objectives such as individualized learning, equality of opportunity, recurrent education, etc. Secondly, it follows that the discussion of structural reform refers not to isolated institutions or separate sectors of higher education but to their interrelationships and to the system as a whole.

In this perspective, following a brief analysis of recent quantitative trends, the problem of post-secondary education structures will be dealt with under three main headings:

    i) the need for an enlargement of the traditional concept of higher education;

    ii) the meaning and practical implications of the concept of diversification; and

    iii) the strategies and processes for bringing about structural change.

2. QUANTITATIVE EXPANSION AND PERSPECTIVES OF FURTHER GROWTH

The quantitative expansion of higher education during the fifties and sixties has been described and analysed in detail in earlier OECD reports. (1) The latest trends are analysed in a special background report to this Conference. (2)   The following Table 1 and graph provide a schematic illustration of this expansion.

Whether or not a similar growth will take place in the seventies is still an open question. Two years ago the Secretariat estimated that further expansion was highly probable - albeit with some fluctuations and possibly at a slower pace than in the past - mainly because of the existence of several important sources of potential growth, i.e.:

    a) enrolment ratios are still relatively low almost everywhere, particularly in the European Member countries;

    b) the trend towards the generalization of secondary education still continues, and this has been up to now the most powerful growth factor in post-secondary education;

    c) disparities in educational participation related to social and regional origin and to sex are still considerable, and policies towards wider and more equal participation will lead inevitably to an increase in global demand for higher education.

These growth potentials have not substantially changed during the past few years. Available statistical data (3) show that in at least nine out of the twenty-four Member countries the growth rates of enrolments in the period 1965 to 1970 remained practically unchanged; they increased in three countries, while in another nine there was a marked slow-down

1. See, in particular, Development of Higher Education 1950-1967: Analytical Report, 1971, and Statistical Survey. 1970, OECD, Paris.

2. See Study I "Quantitative Trends in Post-Secondary Education in OECD Countries, 1960-1970" in "Towards Mass Higher Education: Trends, Issues and Dilemmas", OECD, Paris, 1974.

3. Ibid.

Table 1.   ENROLMENTS IN HIGHER EDUCATION

Thousands

	1950	1960	1965	1970
Austria	22.5	38.9	50.1	62.5
Belgium	30.2	52.0	84.0	127.1*
Denmark	19.5	32.5	53.2	77.1
Finland	17.6	29.2	48.5	67.1
France	185.4	256.0	527.0	778.8[1]
Germany	146.9*	313.2[3]	367.4	494.9
Greece	15.3*	30.5	66.7	84.6[1]
Iceland	0.6*	0.8*	1.1*	1.4*
Ireland	11.2	14.0	20.7	26.2
Italy	240.7	284.3	424.7	694.2
Luxembourg	0.3	0.5	0.7	0.6
Netherlands	63.5*	109.4	152.6	229.5
Norway	13.3	21.7	35.9	49.3
Portugal	14.4	24.0	34.5	52.0
Spain	113.8*	185.4	274.1	351.9
Sweden	27.3	47.9	83.5	145.7
Switzerland	18.3	30.0*	35.0*	43.0[2]
Turkey	27.7	65.4	103.1	155.4
United Kingdom	294.7*	287.7*	433.4*	589.7[1]
Yugoslavia	60.4	140.6	184.9	261.2
Australia	34.9*	70.7	131.7*	175.4
Canada	167.0	286.3	471.3	711.1
Japan	240.0	712.0	1,093.0	1,685.6
USA	2,297.0	3,610.0	5,570.3	7,608.0

*   Estimate.
1.   1969.
2.   1968.
3.   1961.

Source: Ibid.

in expansion over the same period.   In only two countries is it possible
to speak of a stagnation or slight decline in enrolment numbers, and the
overall average annual growth rate for the OECD area remained 7.5%
for 1965-1970 as against 9.1% for 1960-1965.   The demographic factor

INCREASE IN HIGHER EDUCATION ENROLMENTS
FROM 1950/51 TO 1970/71

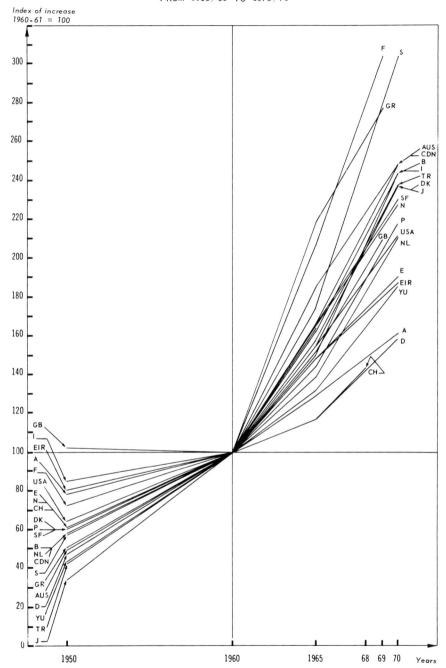

seems to have played a limited role in this sustained growth: in two-thirds of the OECD countries it accounted for less than 30% of the growth rate and for more than 50% in only the United States. Thus, as in the fifties and early sixties, the increase in individual demand for higher education, and the growth in participation rates, have continued to re-present the main factors in the expansion of enrolments.

Even when the latest figures are considered, as in Table 2, there does not appear to be any general slowing down.

Table 2.   RECENT TRENDS IN FLOWS OF NEW ENTRANTS

Average annual growth rates (%)

	1965-70	1968-70	1970-1/1971-2
Austria	5. 4	7. 0	13. 4
Belgium [1]	6. 8	7. 3	6. 4
Denmark	6. 0	10. 6	15. 0
France [1]	9. 5	4. 0	3. 7
Sweden [1]	8. 9	-6	-11
United Kingdom[1]	6. 1	3. 8	3. 5
USA			
- 4-year colleges	2. 4	0. 4	1. 3
- 2-year colleges	9. 1	7. 3	6. 0

1.   Universities only.
Source: Ibid.

In Sweden - the only country in which there has been a decrease in enrolments since 1968 - it is expected that the trend will soon be reversed. National projections for the seventies(1) foresee a generally slower rate of expansion in nine countries, a further acceleration in five countries and a probable stagnation in three. It must be remembered, however, that practically all past projections have represented under-estimations, and for the early seventies this appears again to be the case, for example in Sweden and in Austria. (see Table 3)

It seems, therefore, that if the same factors affecting growth in the sixties continue to operate in the seventies it is reasonable to expect that growth will continue, even if at a slightly slower rate than in the sixties. For the moment at least, there is little to indicate that the ex-pansion will be less than 4 to 6% per annum, which means a further doubl-ing of enrolments within the next 12 to 18 years.

1.   Ibid.

21

Table 3.   AVERAGE ANNUAL GROWTH RATES
OF EXPECTED ENROLMENTS

(Most recent forecasts)

Austria	1960-64 : (2. 5)	Germany	1960-70 : 5. 8
	1970-75 : (5. 2)		1970-75 : 6. 6 (7. 2)
	1975-80 : (7. 8)		1970-85 : (5. 6)
Denmark	1960-70 : 9. 4	Sweden	1960-70 : 12. 7
	1970-84 : 4. 5		1970-74 : -1
Finland	1962-72 : 5. 8	Switzerland	1960-70 : (7. 1)
	1972-75 : 4. 0		1970-75 : (2. 6)
	1975-81 : 7. 8		1975-80 : (1. 6)
France	1960-70 : 10. 8	United Kingdom	1962-71 : 8. 9 (8. 0)
	1970-75 : (3. 8)		1971-80 : 5. 0 (4. 8)
	1970-85 : 2. 8		
Canada	1960-70 : (10. 4)	Japan	1960-70 : 9. 0
	1970-75 : (12. 2)		1971-80 : 4. 1
	1975-80 : (6. 1)		
		United States	1960-70 : 8. 5
			1970-80 : 4. 5

	1960-69	1969-79
Greece	12. 8	5. 5
Portugal	8. 3	8. 7
Spain	9. 4	9. 6
Turkey	11. 2	5. 8
Yugoslavia	6. 9	5. 8

The figures in brackets refer to university type education only.

Source: Ibid.

      The pattern of such expansion will of course be influenced by the impact of new factors affecting the development of the demand for post-secondary education. These include:

    a)   the role of the graduate employment situation as a psychological deterrent or incentive (both in the long and in the short run) to the further expansion of demand. This psychological aspect should be particularly stressed because it is often overlooked that demand is influenced as much by the individual's perception of the labour market situation as by this situation per se. Also it has been clearly established that a particular stage of economic development can imply widely differing capacities of absorption of higher education graduates, depending on the prevailing relations between education and employment;

b) the growth in GNP and the proportion of it devoted to higher education. While the predictions concerning GDP point towards an annual growth of 5. 3% for the period 1970-1980 (for the OECD area as a whole), it is hardly possible to forecast the proportion that will be devoted to higher education because of the essentially political nature of decisions in this matter;

c) the extent to which a system of recurrent education becomes generalized, i. e. a system of "step-outs" (interruption of studies) after secondary education and later "step-ins";

d) the availability of formal post-secondary education opportunities and of informal or "non-traditional" alternatives not accounted for in conventional statistical enrolment data;

e) the effectiveness of various policy measures concerning post-secondary education, particularly as regards meeting the demand from adults.

Whatever view one may take of the relative impact of these factors on the future growth of higher education, it is clear that the quantitative expansion of the fifties and sixties has already led to profound changes in the nature of the different post-secondary systems and in the conditions in which they now have to operate. These are changes which have generated not only quantitatively enlarged systems but systems which are different in kind.

3.   NEW GOALS AND NEW TENSIONS

Expansion was not the only factor which generated these changes. In the first place, the goal structure of post-secondary systems has been enlarged. Society today expects higher education to fulfil a wider number of functions than those assigned to it in the past. In addition to the transmission and extension of knowledge (teaching and research), modern systems of post-secondary education are required in particular:

a) to play an important role in the general social objective of achieving greater equality of opportunity;

b) to provide education adapted to a great diversity of individual qualifications, motivations, expectations and career aspirations;

c) to facilitate the process of lifelong learning;

d) to assume a "public service function", i. e. to make a contribution to the solution of major problems faced by the community surrounding the higher education institution and by society at large, and to participate directly in the process of social change.

This new goal structure for post-secondary education, superimposed on its traditional functions, gives rise to a number of critical areas of tension around which much of the current debate on the future of higher education revolves. Such tensions exist, for example:

- between the requirements of excellence and of egalitarianism;
- between the structure and size of individual demand for higher education and of labour market requirements;
- between the aspirations and interests of the different groups involved in higher education;
- between the aspirations and expectations of individuals and the prevailing socio-economic constraints in terms of availability of resources, academic attitudes, institutional hierarchies, established cultural and social value structures striving for self-perpetuation.

As in other areas of social life such conflicts are not necessarily destructive per se. In fact, the continuous interplay of antagonistic forces can provide the indispensable condition for change and innovation. The question therefore is whether out of these growing conflicts and tensions post-secondary systems can evolve the necessary mechanisms and structural adjustments which would lead to a succession of creative responses rather than to a blockage in the functioning of the system itself.

TOWARDS A SYSTEM OF "POST-COMPULSORY" EDUCATION

1. THE OVERALL CONCEPT

From a strictly quantitative point of view, it is now clear that the expansion of higher education in the fifties and sixties was conditioned to a great extent by the development of secondary education and that the two growth curves are definitely correlated. (1) The qualitative implications of this relation are no less obvious. As shown in one of the Conference reports, (2) the whole process of access to higher education, especially in Europe, is largely determined by the traditional function of the secondary school as a selection mechanism and by the key impact which this has on the nature, characteristics and qualifications of the student body entering higher education. This explains why various policy measures designed to achieve greater equality of educational opportunity at the higher education level (decentralization of institutions, student grants, loans, etc.) have so far had only limited effect, and why in spite of the very rapid growth of enrolments social disparities have remained considerable. Similarly, the whole numerus clausus/open access debate will remain to a great extent artificial unless the more fundamental problem is solved of deciding among which groups of the population selection should take place and who should benefit from open access to higher education. Finally, the close relation between secondary and post-secondary education is also clearly reflected in the curriculum: what is offered at the higher education level, especially during the first two years, must be closely related to the nature of the qualifications, motivations and expectations of the student population leaving secondary school.

It is probably in this link that the crucial issue resides. It poses in fact the whole problem of the goals of secondary education as it exists today and of the options available to the 16-19 age group. If these options continue to imply, as they do at present, irreversible choices between work and higher education, or a segregation between vocationally (work) oriented and further study (university) oriented education, any policy aimed at establishing a more equitable system of higher education can have but very limited effect.

For all these reasons a new articulation between upper secondary and post-secondary education becomes an issue of utmost importance calling for the development of a coherent system of post-compulsory education covering all forms of educational activity after the end of compulsory schooling, one which would include upper secondary education

---

1. Cf. Table 6.
2. See Study II "Admission Policies in Post-Secondary Education" in "Towards Mass Higher Education - Trends, Issues and Dilemmas", OECD, Paris, 1974.

as well as post-secondary, higher and university education proper. Such an approach is also a sine qua non for the progressive generalization of any system of lifelong or recurrent education.

The true point of departure for such a system is the simultaneous opening of the present systems of higher education to four categories of student:

a) graduates of upper secondary education - 17 to 20 years old;
b) those without full upper secondary education qualifications but with practical work experience - 17 to 20 years old;
c) graduates of upper secondary education who have interrupted their formal education and are re-entering the formal education system after a period of work - over 20 to 25 years old;
d) those without full upper secondary education but with a long work experience - over 20 to 25 years old.

Future systems of post-secondary education will have to respond to the demands of a variety of groups of students differing radically in age, qualifications, motivations and expectations. This implies the need to consider as an interrelated whole all formal education and all education-work combinations between the end of compulsory schooling and graduate education, including evening courses for adults. In the last analysis, it is only within such an enlarged framework that most of the important issues in higher education can be intelligibly analysed and effective policy measures taken. The examination of such key problems as equality of opportunity and selection acquires a new significance if undertaken in the light of this enlarged concept of post-compulsory education.

2. EQUALITY OF OPPORTUNITY

The prevailing disparities in the participation rates of different social groups in post-secondary systems have been widely discussed both in national and international reports. (1)   Though it is recognized that growth alone does not lead automatically to a diminishing of these disparities, the latest available figures show that the expansion of the sixties has had some impact on the social composition of the student body. Table 4 shows that although the chances of gaining access to university for students from the under-privileged classes are still considerably lower than those of students from the upper social strata (five times less in the best case in Western Europe), there has been a considerable improvement almost everywhere over the period 1960-1970.

There are however several reasons why this trend should not be regarded as necessarily providing an eventual solution to the problem. First, it is far from certain that a kind of ceiling does not exist beyond which the existing structures will not allow further progress. Secondly, the pace of progress is rather slow and may therefore not be politically acceptable. Thirdly, and most important, in most cases the equalization trend as reflected in the overall figures conceals new types of disparities - for example, in rates of achievement - which modern societies will find as objectionable as those arising from an inequality in the global

1.   See Group Disparities in Educational Participation and Achievement. Conference on Policies for Educational Growth, Vol. IV, OECD, Paris 1971.

Table 4.   RELATIVE CHANCES OF UPPER STRATUM
AND LOWER STRATUM YOUTH OF STUDYING IN A UNIVERSITY

France	1959	84:1	U.K. (England)	1961	8:1
	1964	30:1	and Wales)	1970	5:1
	1968	28:1			
Germany	1961	58:1	Sweden	1960	9:1
	1964	48:1		1968	5:1
	1970	12:1			
Netherlands..	1961	56:1	Yugoslavia...	1960	6:1
	1964	45:1		1965	4:1
	1970	26:1		1969	3.5:1

Source: Study I in 'Towards Mass Higher Education ...'. op. cit.

participation rates. Thus, drop-out rates among students of modest
origin are higher than among those from middle and upper classes. The
latter groups, furthermore, continue to be heavily over-represented in
certain fields of study or institutions (usually the prestigious institutions
with selective admission procedures) which open up particularly promising career prospects, while the former concentrate in areas and institutions providing, in general, entry into less privileged occupations.

Table 5.   PERCENTAGE OF STUDENTS
FROM LOWER SOCIO-ECONOMIC GROUP

	UNIVERSITIES	SHORT-CYCLE INSTITUTIONS
Canada		
– Ontario (1968)	26.7	40.0 (CAAT)
– Quebec	24.9	38.3 (CEGEP)
France (1968)	11.9	24.2 (IUT)
United Kingdom (1961)	26.0	37.9 (non-university institutions)
(1970)	27.0	36.0 (5 polytechnics)
USA (1966)	11.0	18.0 (2-year colleges)
Yugoslavia (1970)	17.0	22.0 (Više Škole)

Source: Ibid.

Such new disparities are also reflected in the structure of the post-secondary system itself. Until now practically no strategy for the diversification of higher education has been able to overcome a certain division of the education system into a "noble" and a "less noble" sector, with all its important social and educational implications. While in the past this situation could have been justified on the grounds that it facilitated the access of middle and lower strata students to post-secondary education, this differentiation is likely to be increasingly questioned in the future. The figures showing the percentage of students from lower classes in short-cycle and non-university higher education and the corresponding figures for universities eloquently illustrate this point.

A further disparity to which increasing attention is now being paid concerns the so-called "generation gap". In Sweden, two-thirds of the present adult population had only six to seven years of formal schooling while today nearly 90% of the young people obtain at least eleven years of formal education. (1) Equality of opportunity is increasingly seen in the context of the right of adults, as well as of the young, to benefit from educational facilities spread over a longer span in the life cycle.

The general conclusions which can be drawn from the above may be summarized as follows. The post-secondary systems of practically all Member countries have undergone a process of democratization in the last decade, but at the same time these systems have developed more subtle socially-biased selection mechanisms. The growing awareness that traditional measures are insufficient to push the process beyond a certain ceiling, and that they even give rise to new types of disparities, points to the need for new, more imaginative and comprehensive measures. The effectiveness of such measures will depend to a large extent on their ability to encompass the overall structures of post-compulsory education and to bring about, as a matter of public policy, closer affiliation of formal and informal education. (2)

Certain elements of such policies are already emerging and are reflected in actual trends:

    i) a trend towards comprehensive secondary education and/or the disappearance of a hierarchy between the various types of secondary education, all of which are to provide access to post-secondary education, including university;

    ii) a trend towards allowing access to post-secondary education to those who have not terminated secondary education;

    iii) a trend towards developing non-traditional forms of study at post-secondary level for those whose formal qualifications, motivations and life situations differ from those of the traditional type of entrant into higher education.

The first of these three trends, analysed in detail in one of the Conference reports, (3) is linked to the traditional relationship between secondary and higher education which has dominated the European scene during the past decades: the growth of secondary education has been the main precondition and direct cause of the expansion of higher education. (4)

1. See "Admission Policies in Swedish Post-Secondary Education", internal OECD document, Paris, 1973 (mimeo.).

2. This is not to underestimate the crucial role of measures taken in secondary, primary and pre-primary education in the pursuit of equality of educational opportunity, but clearly this does not constitute a sufficient reason for any government to abrogate its responsibilities for specific measures at the post-compulsory level to attenuate the effects of existing disparities.

3. See Study II in "Towards Mass Higher Education ...", op. cit.

4. See Development of Higher Education 1950-1967: Analytical Report, op. cit.

Beyond its quantitative implications, this direct influence, especially in continental Europe, has been the main determinant of the social composition of the student body in higher education. Since up to 90% of academic (general) secondary school graduates transferred to university, and since graduates of other types of secondary schools were in effect unqualified to enter university, the social origin of students in European universities could be only a replica of the social composition prevailing in general secondary schools. For this reason alone, measures taken at only the higher education level necessarily had very little effect, and any real improvement would logically have required that the universities be opened to graduates of broader categories of secondary schools where students from lower classes have a higher rate of participation. This has happened in several European countries, e.g. Austria, Belgium, Italy, Yugoslavia.

The move towards comprehensive secondary schools in a few European countries, particularly in Scandinavia, represented a more radical solution to the problem, but it is still too early to draw any conclusions from this experience.

It may well be that considering the inevitably slow pace of change in education and in the attitudes of social groups, the effects of measures at the secondary school level will not be fully felt for at least another decade. If this is the case, a substantial increase in equality of opportunity at the higher education level cannot take place before quasi-universal or mass secondary education has been achieved, that is before 70 to 80% of the age group succeed in terminating secondary school, as is already the case in the United States, Canada, Japan and the USSR. Until now, mass higher education has always been a concomitant of generalized secondary education, (1) as Table 6 shows.

It can be seen from this table that most of the European rates are still so low that it will be many years before 70 to 80% enrolment is achieved at upper secondary level. (Only Sweden expects to reach a ratio of about 90% in the coming years.) But the pressure for a better representation of the lower classes in higher education is such that no government will find it easy to delay progress over such a long period.

It has been partly in response to these difficulties that the second trend has emerged, namely allowing access to post-secondary education to those without full secondary education and the development of non-traditional forms of study. The British Open University, the American Empire State College, the City University of New York, and the Swedish 25/5 scheme are among the best-known examples of this trend, which, significantly enough, appears on both sides of the Atlantic. (2) In other words, countries at completely different stages of development of their higher and secondary education systems - those with 15% higher education enrolment and 30% secondary enrolment ratios, and those with more than 40% and 70% respectively - are in search of the same type of policies and the same structural features of "non-traditional" higher education. Following Martin Trow's concept of three stages in the development of higher education - elite/mass/universal(3) - it can be said, at least with respect to this phenomenon, that a certain telescoping of the stages takes place, "elite" systems trying to acquire some features of the "universal access" systems without passing through the "mass" stage, that is without waiting for the advent of mass secondary education.

1. "Towards New Structures of Post-Secondary Education", op. cit., p. 33.

2. See "New Approaches in Post-Secondary Education", OECD Document, Paris, 1974.

3. See Part One, section III, of the present volume.

Table 6. NUMBERS OF SECONDARY SCHOOL-LEAVING CERTIFICATES
AS A PERCENTAGE OF THE POPULATION
OF THE CORRESPONDING AGE GROUP (Column 1)
AND ENROLMENT RATIOS IN HIGHER EDUCATION (Column II)

(1965 or 1966)

	I	II
Austria	11. 7	7. 5
Belgium	29. 6	14. 9
France	17. 4	17. 4
Italy	18. 0	11. 3
Netherlands	18. 8	13. 6
Spain	6. 6	8. 7
Sweden	18. 5	13. 1
Switzerland	4. 3	7. 7
United Kingdom	18. 7	11. 9
Yugoslavia	21. 0	13. 1
Canada	71. 6	23. 7
Japan	50. 5	12. 0
United States	75. 7	40. 8
USSR	58. 4	31. 0
- of which full-time		12. 7

Source: Development of Higher Education 1950-1967: Analytical Report, op. cit.

This might be a significant phenomenon because it implies that European
development may not necessarily follow the same sequence as that exemplified by the American system.

It is as yet early to assess how the opening of higher education to
those without full secondary education and the development of non-traditional forms of study are contributing to equalizing educational opportunity. Such information as is available points at first sight to a rather
negative conclusion: the percentage of people from the working classes in
the British Open University is lower than in the traditional universities
and the great majority of those benefiting from the 25/5 scheme in Sweden
seem to have secondary school qualifications which would enable them to
enter university in any case. It can be argued, however, that this is due
both to the newness of these schemes and to the statistical procedures
used: in traditional higher education, students are classified according to
the socio-economic status of their fathers; in non-traditional forms they

are classified according to their own status with no consideration given to the possibility that many belonging to middle class professions might come from working class families.

The growth of non-traditional access routes to higher education both responds to and generates a new demand for higher education in quantitative terms and in terms of the range of qualifications and expectations of those entering post-secondary institutions. It is this new demand that lies behind the third trend mentioned above, namely the adaptation of the content and methods of post-secondary education to the qualifications, motivations and life situations of the "non-traditional" students. This implies, for example, setting up course timetables suitable for those continuing their employment, the creation of regional ("off campus") centres with the necessary facilities (library, guidance services, audio and video equipment, etc.) and, above all, new curricula responsive to the kinds of experiences, qualifications and aspirations which the new students bring with them. The implications of the concept of "the new student" are yet to be investigated in all their ramifications: this would require, for example, the use of surveys on potential and actual "clients" of the non-traditional forms of education and might extend to a study of certification methods of relevant work experience and self-education. Schemes which are already well established, such as the French CNAM(1) and the External Degree in the United Kingdom, deserve to be analysed in depth for the guidance they could provide for future developments, particularly in the context of their possible integration into the emerging network of new non-traditional post-secondary institutions and thus into the overall system of post-secondary education. Though many existing schemes were conceived in a different perspective - set up essentially as ad hoc compensatory measures in response to the specific needs of certain social groups - the new trend in the development of non-traditional patterns of learning sees them as a significant characteristic of the whole system. In this respect, new programmes such as the Extended University of the University of California(2) will represent particularly valuable testing grounds because they aim at the penetration of a network of prestigious establishments by a system of new educational patterns, rather than the creation of a non-traditional institution parallel to an existing one. Most probably the key problem in using non-traditional forms of post-secondary education as a tool in the equalization of opportunity will be precisely this penetration of the overall system, the main challenge being to avoid a new split between "noble" traditional and "less noble" non-traditional patterns of higher education.

Conceptually, a comprehensive system of recurrent education, (3) that is a system based on the alternation of periods of study and work beginning at the end of compulsory schooling and continuing through the life-span of the individual, might represent the only fully satisfactory solution to this problem. The progressive creation of such a system might however raise the same dilemmas as those discussed in relation to short-cycle higher education, (4) that is, a polarization of institutions and patterns set up on the recurrent education principle and of those which continue to follow the more or less traditional rules, the former becoming

1. "Conservatoire national des arts et métiers".

2. Cf. "A Strategy for Change in Higher Education: The Extended University of the University of California", OECD Document, Paris, 1974.

3. Cf. Recurrent Education: A Strategy for Lifelong Learning. CERI/OECD, Paris, 1973.

4. Short-Cycle Higher Education: A Search for Identity, OECD, Paris, 1973.

automatically the "less noble" sector of higher education and the latter persisting as its prestigious and status-generating component. The key practical question, therefore, is which post-secondary education structures would (a) facilitate the advent of recurrent education but at the same time (b) prevent a new split in the system. Most of the considerations in the present report address themselves ultimately to providing the key elements of an answer to this question.

3. SELECTION

The issue of equality of opportunity leads inevitably to consideration of selection problems, which are in turn closely linked to questions of resource allocation, costs and financial constraints.

Clearly, cost and financing considerations are the dominant feature of the present public debate on growth and reform of post-secondary education. As shown in one of the Conference reports,(1) the percentage of GNP devoted to higher education has more than doubled in most Member countries over the past decade. In general, this expenditure has also increased much more rapidly than both expenditure on other educational sectors and total government expenditure. This disproportionate growth of higher education expenditure is at least in part a consequence of the fact that the growth of productivity in higher education is almost inevitably slower than in the economy at large, which leads to a continuous increase in unit costs, an increase which can be expected to continue in the future. This, together with a change in the climate of opinion on the usefulness of continued growth in higher education, and the competing demand on resources from other social sectors (health, environment, transport, etc.), often leads to the policy conclusion that stricter selection measures must sooner or later be imposed on those wishing to enter higher education.

This situation calls for two general comments. First, it is difficult to say at which point a real ceiling is reached in the proportion of GNP (or of total government expenditure) devoted to higher education. In 1970 this proportion varied from 0.7% in Norway and Germany to 2.7% in Canada, most of the European countries being close to 1%. In economic terms it cannot be shown why these countries could not continue to increase their expenditure on higher education for a relatively long period, or even why North America could not go beyond the present 2.5 to 3.0% figures.

However, this is clearly not an economic issue but a question of political priorities. Secondly, and more important, it must be recognized that every system, whatever its stage of development, implies an in-built selection process. The core of the problem for the future is whether this process can operate without the strong social bias which has characterized it in the past. In fact, the argument can be taken further by advocating new and stricter types of selection procedures (e. g. numerus clausus, quotas, positive discrimination) in order to achieve greater equality of educational opportunity. In practice this has already been the case for quite a long time in Eastern European countries where children from working class families enjoy certain formal privileges over their

---

1. See Study IV "The Cost and Finance of Post-Secondary Education" in "Towards Mass Higher Education: Trends, Issues and Dilemmas", op. cit.

peers from middle class families when trying to enter a university. In a different context, the recent Swedish proposals directed towards bridging the educational disparities between generations may be interpreted as another form of positive discrimination. (1) Similarly, recent developments in the United States have led to a situation today in which students from minority ethnic groups can get into college - especially into the most prestigious ones - with fewer formal qualifications than students from other social groups. (2)

The real issue therefore is not open access versus selection, but a question of which selection criteria and mechanisms would be the most appropriate for the future. That is why the distinction between systems in which universities select their students and those which have to accept everyone who has appropriate secondary school qualifications implies merely a distinction between systems with different strategic points and modes of selection. (3)

The main problem here is the particular position of universities or, more exactly, of institutions which in the existing systems are associated with a special, almost sacrosanct function any change in which would be considered unacceptable. If Harvard, the Massachusetts Institute of Technology, Oxford or the University of Moscow made their admission criteria even more strict than they are already, very few would resent it; if French, German or Italian universities tried to impose a selective admission procedure, a major revolution might take place. In a sense, therefore, it can be said that the strategic points and modes of selection are to a great extent historically and sociologically rooted, if not determined. The special place and role of the universities within the global post-secondary system must be seen in this perspective, and any reforms of the existing selection processes both within and outside universities must consider the unavoidable resistances which even the most rational plans will raise.

In almost all Member countries the main deficiency of the traditional selection processes is their rather rigid and irreversible nature and the fact that they are based on a very limited number of criteria, among which the distinction between academic and vocational education and between formal education and work has a preeminent place. In fact, almost every existing post-secondary system consists of a mixture of relatively selective and non-selective institutions: open and numerus clausus faculties in Scandinavia, universities and "grandes écoles" in France, Further Education Colleges and universities in the United Kingdom, Junior Colleges and prestigious universities in the United States, etc. This means that even systems considered by the public as open, such as those of continental Europe, are in fact only relatively open in one of their sectors; and the relative openness of one sector leads almost inevitably to greater selection in another. At times this quasi-spontaneous process produces rather paradoxical results: for example, universities in France and Germany are not selective but non-university institutions providing education below degree level (IUTs, "Fachochschulen") do apply selection procedures.

One final point should be stressed. Any selection process - whether at the level of a particular institution or at the level of the system - has its formal (manifest) and informal (latent) aspects. This is particularly

1. Cf. "Admission Policies in Swedish Post-Secondary Education", op. cit.

2. This is certainly one of the reasons why black enrolments in American higher education between 1970 and 1971 increased by 17% as against 4.1% for total enrolments.

3. Cf. Study II in "Towards Mass Higher Education ...", op. cit.

true of "selection by failure" during the course of higher education. In most of the continental European countries this kind of selection eliminates 40 to 60% of new entrants, which to a large extent makes all formal selection measures, as well as policies designed to open the system, of rather limited significance. Future systems of post-secondary education will also have to consider the selection process, though not necessarily from this point of view. As will be shown in the last part of this paper, and as recent events in several European countries have demonstrated, the main practical difficulty here lies in the attitudes of the various social groups, not least the members of the academic community, including the student body. Many of them seem in fact to accept various concealed selection measures - even though very drastic and socially unjust - more easily than they accept any openly-stated new selection criteria.

THE IMPLICATIONS OF DIVERSIFICATION

1.   THE INEVITABILITY OF DIVERSIFICATION

Few concepts in the field of education encounter such general acceptance as that of diversification of post-secondary education. Diversification is advocated as a remedy to almost every problem faced by existing higher education systems, whether in the field of curriculum reform, methods of study, degree structure, organisation of courses or institutional framework. Many see diversification as an objective in itself consequent on the acceptance of a pluralistic society; others tend to see it as a protective measure for shielding elitist institutions from the onslaught of mass higher education.

The arguments usually advanced in favour of diversification are the following:

- the increasingly heterogeneous student clientele of higher education with its diversity of motivations, aptitudes, qualifications and aspirations;
- the growing needs of the economy and society for a diversity of skills and qualifications;
- the multiplicity of functions which the institutions and systems of post-secondary education are expected to assume;
- the desire for more individualized and student-centred education;
- the need for flexibility of the system, which a unidimensional structure cannot provide.

It is generally admitted that the existing systems are not sufficiently diversified inasmuch as "they offer only a small number of possibilities of access (usually through a single specific type of secondary school), only one or a very limited number of patterns of study (with respect to duration, types of attendance, kinds of degrees awarded) and a relatively small and rather rigidly fixed number of fields of study. This homogeneity is obviously in contradiction with the wide range of abilities, interests and motivations of the extended student population, as well as with the increased diversity of skills and qualifications required by modern economies."(1)

Diversification, consequently, implies an increased number of educational offerings, means of access, patterns of study, and degrees and ways in which to obtain them.

It can also be assumed that the degree of diversification of a given system corresponds to a large extent to its stage of quantitative and

---

1.   "Towards New Structures of Post-Secondary Education", op.cit., pp. 28-29.

qualitative development. Thus, elite higher education, being dominated by a single institutional type - that is, the traditional university and its standards and values - is characterized by an undifferentiated structure or, at best, one based on the "binary" principle. Mass higher education, on the other hand, is much more diversified because of the existence of a large number of institutional types and educational patterns, though this does not necessarily mean that the characteristics of the earlier binary stage disappear altogether. This conceptual framework helps to relate the development of higher education to a phenomenon which is found in all social systems whose evolution is characterized by "an increasing differentiation of structure and increasing specialization of function". (1)

The trend towards diversification might thus appear to be practically unavoidable and as natural a development in higher education as in any other sector of society. Yet, experience shows that quite often the educational sub-system moves in this direction at only a very slow pace and can even be temporarily blocked. A situation of conflict consequently arises between a highly differentiated society and a much less differentiated higher education system. The main question therefore is not so much whether diversification will take place, but whether it will not lag too far behind the diversification process in other social sub-systems.

Looking at past patterns of development in individual countries, a clear distinction can be made between those which have already reached very high enrolment ratios at the post-secondary level (United States, USSR and, more recently, Canada) and most of the others. Both in the United States and in the USSR this more rapid growth of the systems was accompanied, or even preceded, by a diversification of post-secondary structures. In this sense the United States has for a long time had a system which facilitated the advent of mass higher education. "In fact, elements of such structures have probably existed in the USA since the end of the 19th century: diversification of curriculum, service function of universities (Land Grant Colleges), mobility of students. It could possibly be argued that these elements contributed to the relatively high enrolment ratios already reached in the United States many years ago (in 1965 no European country had ratios which America had reached in 1950). "(2) In the case of the USSR, too, the creation of its post-secondary system with a multitude of institutional types and educational patterns - universities, technical institutions, evening and correspondence courses - preceded and facilitated the large quantitative expansion.

Conversely, in most of the European countries, the great increase in enrolments, especially in most recent years, seems almost always to have preceded diversification measures. In other words, diversification constituted a growth factor in the first group of countries, while the reverse was true in Europe.

1.   Robert Marsh, Comparative Sociology, Harcourt, Brace and World, New York, 1967, p. 31. The author develops this point by showing that differentiation - a term which might be used interchangeably with diversification - should be considered both as a state and as a process. "As a state, differentiation can be defined as the number of structurally distinct and functionally specialized units in society"; as a process, it means "the emergence of more distinct organs to fulfill more distinct functions", or "as the process of multiplications of one structural unit of a society into two or more structural units that function more effectively in the changed functional exigencies of the situation".

2.   "Towards New Structures of Post-Secondary Education", op. cit., p. 32.

It is difficult to assess at which point a gap between the degree of diversification of post-secondary education and that of other social sectors becomes critical. But, clearly, such situations already exist and lead to a certain blocking of the system, which has at least two important consequences. On the one hand, society (and the economy in particular) in order to meet new needs generates new forms of post-secondary education outside the formal system, with the result that graduates of the latter suffer from increased unemployment or under-employment, sometimes even in situations of quasi-full employment. Secondly, the traditional, undiversified structure under increased pressure may find it impossible to fulfil adequately even those goals and functions in the name of which it resisted diversification, namely maintaining standards of "excellence" and contributing to the advancement of knowledge.

2.   PATTERNS OF DIVERSIFICATION

A meaningful discussion of the actual and desirable forms of diversification might best be undertaken by focussing successively on a number of major aspects of the functioning of higher education. These are:

a)   access,
b)   curriculum and structure of studies,
c)   length and methods of studies, modes of attendance, and
d)   the institutional framework.

a)   Access(1)

Diversification of access implies the existence of a multiplicity of routes allowing entry into post-secondary education: successful termination of general as well as of vocational secondary education, various types of qualifications acquired in employment, individual study outside formal schools, different kinds of professional training and remedial courses, etc. In most Member countries, all or most of these different access routes are already either fully authorized or are being introduced on an experimental basis. At least three aspects of the new multiple access schemes call for particular attention:

  i)   several of the new access routes remain virtually unused for a long time after they are formally opened. This is often due to the fact that their introduction is not accompanied by measures designed to overcome latent but nonetheless real obstacles, and also because of the inherent inertia of social behaviour. In the late sixties, in the majority of countries, less than 5% of university entrants lacked the traditional secondary school qualifications;(2)
 ii)   methods of determining admission qualifications for those using non-traditional access routes (work experience, individual study outside school) are still uncertain and often quite arbitrary;
iii)   the multiplication of access routes leads sometimes to a rather complex system in which each of these different routes allows

---

1.   See also the earlier section on Selection, p. 32.
2.   See Study I in "Towards Mass Higher Education...", op. cit., Table 20.

admission to only one post-secondary education institution or course (or to a very limited number). This could easily lead to a new, more or less rigid hierarchy of access routes which, as already mentioned, might in turn lead to new educational disparities.

A fourth consideration might be added: for the moment there is an almost total lack of adequate information on the problems and achievements of students who enter the system through the non-traditional routes. Some of the recent pilot experiments, such as the Open University or the Swedish 25/5 scheme, are probably too new to allow such assessment. Others, however, have existed for a sufficiently long time to provide very useful information: for example in Yugoslavia, the City University of New York or students admitted to the University of Vincennes in France without the traditional baccalauréat, and not forgetting the very successful experience with World War II veterans.

b) Curriculum, structure of studies and the place of research in higher education

Diversification of the curriculum in post-secondary education relates above all to the range of fields of study offered. This range can be as narrow as the medieval trivium and quadrivium or as wide as in the present American system where degrees can be obtained in some 1,600 fields of study. Here again, there seems to be a close historical correlation between the general development of higher education and the progressive diversification of the curriculum. In the American system, a major breakthrough in this process took place as early as the second part of the 19th century, after the creation of the Land Grant Colleges. European universities followed much later and opened themselves to new "non-established" disciplines and problem-oriented fields of study only after the Second World War, sometimes even as late as the sixties. Today the principle of diversification is generally accepted, although it is still sometimes considerably easier to introduce new, as yet academically unrecognized fields of study into the non-university sector of higher education (either in existing institutions or by creating new ones) than into the universities (as was the case with technological fields 50 to 100 years ago). In other words, it often appears easier to establish inter-institutional diversification of curriculum than intra-institutional. It must be noted, however, that a certain reaction is developing against offering too wide a range of fields of study. Thus, the Carnegie Commission recommends "that the 1,600 current degrees be reduced to 160 at the most", (1) and that several curriculum reforms should envisage less numerous and broader areas of study (at least at the first level of higher education) in order to give the graduate a wider range of career options and to make higher education more polyvalent. In a sense, a search for the modern equivalent of the trivium or quadrivium may be said to be under way and the diversification of curriculum seems to have reached its ceiling. The implications of this trend clearly relate, on the one hand, to the whole issue of interdisciplinary studies and, on the other, to the concept of a "common core" of studies both in relation to academic preparation and to the needs of groups of professions. The issues involved

_____

1. Less Time, More Options, Carnegie Commission on Higher Education, McGraw-Hill, Hightstown, N.Y., 1971.

in these developments have been analysed in detail elsewhere (1) and only their structural implications need be raised here.

There are two possibilities: the creation of new "interdisciplinary institutions" or special establishments providing common core studies; or the introduction of these studies within existing institutions. Both alternatives are being considered and which is adopted will largely depend on circumstances and on local conditions and traditions. Examples of the first approach are the Green Bay College, Wisconsin, where all courses are centred on environmental studies, the University Institute of European Studies in Florence and the College of Europe in Bruges where teaching and research are focussed on problems of European co-operation, and several "Health Universities" (e. g. Haceteppe in Turkey). The second approach is illustrated by a number of the new British and renovated French universities in which the traditional organisation based on disciplinary units (departments or faculties) is replaced by a horizontal division into problem oriented units. But the generalization of both these alternatives comes up against the ingrained preferences of teachers as well as of students who continue to seek recognition and status through traditional disciplinary research and study rather than through participation in interdisciplinary and general education ventures which are often criticized for their apparently "superficial" nature. These problems will not be overcome until higher education institutions undertake in-depth analysis of both the conceptual and practical problems of interdisciplinarity and of its real impact on teaching and research adapted to changes in both knowledge and society.

An important aspect of curriculum diversification relates to the whole problem of the structure of studies, that is, to "the most appropriate sequences and relationships between general and specialized education, between theoretical and practical instruction, and also between formal education and work experience ... It may well be that this is the most crucial issue with regard to the future of higher education, on which all the others in a sense depend, because its solution will, in the final instance, determine the flows of students to and from higher education and their mobility between different educational institutions and between education and work. "(2)

Traditional pedagogy postulated only unilateral relationships and flows from general to specialized, from abstract and theoretical to practical, and from education to job. For a number of reasons reactions against the exclusive place of this pedagogy have multiplied during recent years. First, because, based as it is on the concept of a rigid division between vocational- and work-related education on the one hand and academic education on the other, it does not recognize that individuals seek self-development in different ways and that this must be reflected in the organisation of the educational process. Secondly, it hinders the development of a system of recurrent education based on alternation between work and study. Thirdly, it implies an educational structure which, even though institutionally diversified, is characterized by fragmentation, disconnection and blind alleys.

As several of the Conference reports show, (3) Member countries are tending to adopt two kinds of solution:

1. Interdisciplinarity: Problems of Teaching and Research in Universities, CERI/OECD, Paris, 1972.

2. "Towards New Structures of Post-Secondary Education", op. cit., p. 43.

3. Cf. Study I "New Teaching-Research Relationships in Mass Post-Secondary Education"; Study III "The Integration of Learning and Research in Mass Higher Education: Towards a New Concept of Science"; and Study IV "The American Academic Credit System", in Structure of Studies and Place of Research in Mass Higher Education, OECD, Paris, 1974. See also "Admission Policies in Swedish Post-Secondary Education", op. cit.

    i) combining vocational courses or training with general and
       academic education and, conversely, including more general
       and theoretical education in work-related training;
   ii) organising the educational sequence into small units or modules
       which allow a variety of combinations according to the interests
       and possibilities of the student, thereby creating a kind of
       common currency which makes it possible to transfer the units
       between institutions, fields and levels of study, and possibly
       even between countries.

This latter solution does not necessarily imply a trend towards a
generalization of the credit point system as it operates in the United
States,(1) but it does use two of its components, namely the system of
electives, and inter-institutional transferability enlarged by the concept
of credit for work experience. Such a system could certainly facilitate
the individualization of education and could also provide an appropriate
basis for recurrent education. It does have some drawbacks, however,
in particular the danger that it might lead to fragmentation of knowledge
and favour implicitly only highly motivated students from middle and upper classes to the detriment of vocationally oriented, working class students.(2)   Diversification must necessarily provide for alternative structures of studies and no single model of curriculum can be applied throughout the system.

Closely related to problems of curriculum and structure of studies
are those posed by the place of research in future structures of post-
secondary education. Several, partly conflicting trends can be discerned:

    i) the preeminence of research and of its requirements over
       teaching (in terms of resources, staff and status considera-
       tions). This trend, which developed strongly in the sixties,
       is for a number of reasons being increasingly questioned;(3)
   ii) emigration of research from universities;
  iii) new emphasis on unity of teaching and research, especially
       in "socially-relevant" fields, and on the pedagogical implica-
       tions of research.

Here again, the problem is how to set up structures which allow a
variety of patterns of teaching-research relationships: institutions with
a heavy research component, those with emphasis on "teaching through
research", those assuming more traditional teaching functions, etc.
The main problem is that research activities provide both the institutions
and the people involved with a social status which mere teaching lacks.
As a result, the system, although diversified, becomes hierarchical according to a single, rather rigid norm. Several of the new non-university
institutions endeavour to overcome this trend by allowing their teaching
staff to participate in university research and, in particular, by fostering
various types of applied and other research connected with their local or
regional responsibilities (Norwegian Regional Colleges). It remains to be
seen whether these measures will be sufficient or whether a more fundamental change of the basic underlying values of the system is necessary
before any rigid status hierarchy can be eliminated. It is certain that a
clearcut differentiation between fundamental and applied research (with
all its status connotations) can no longer be maintained, either from an

1. Cf. Study IV in Structure of Studies .... op. cit.
2. Cf. Section III of the "Guidelines for Discussion", Part Two of the present volume.
3. Cf. Study I and Study II in Structure of Studies ...., op. cit.

epistemological or from a practical point of view.   Whether the same is true of research in the sense of advancement of knowledge (both fundamental and applied), of socially-relevant research and research as a pedagogical device, is a debatable point.

c)   Length and methods of study, and modes of attendance

The trend towards diversification presupposes the availability of educational patterns with different lengths and methods of study and different modes of attendance.   This is the reason for the creation and/or extension of short-cycle higher education opportunities in the majority of Member countries through the development of new institutions outside the university sector and, in a smaller number of cases, of new types of courses inside universities. (1)   It is now clear that in most European countries this trend has so far lacked the dynamism which policy-makers may originally have expected of it.   From 1960 to 1965 the annual growth rate of enrolments in non-university establishments in Europe (which, except for the United Kingdom, can be assimilated to short-cycle higher education) was 9.5%, as against 8.9% in universities.   From 1965 to 1970, however, the former rate dropped to 5.6%, which means that the relative power of attraction of short-cycle higher education decreased(2) and that traditional long university studies maintained their dominant position. Interestingly enough, the opposite was true in non-European countries where enrolments in short-cycle institutions (mainly junior and community colleges) continued throughout the sixties and the early seventies to represent the fastest growing sector of post-secondary education: 11.9% per annum for the period 1960-1965 and 11.5% per annum for 1965-1970, as against 8.6% and 6.1%, respectively, for institutions offering long-cycle studies.
The discrepancy between continental Europe on the one hand and the non-European countries on the other is certainly in part due to the different type of functions assigned to short-cycle institutions in each area: in the latter countries they usually represent the open-access sector while in continental Europe they are often more selective than the universities. (3)   This leads to one of the most important issues facing European countries as they enter the stage of mass higher education, namely how to provide opportunities for shorter higher education studies and make them meaningful and acceptable alternatives to a wide range of students. (4)   There appear   to be three possible solutions:

   i) European countries could follow a pattern similar to the American model by developing separate institutions providing both terminal qualifications and qualifications for further study;
  ii) they could set up a polyvalent first stage of higher education within universities;
 iii) they could set up a system of small learning units which would help to blur the distinction between short- and long-cycle higher education by leaving it to the student to decide when to "step out" of the system.

1.   For an extensive analysis of this subject, see Short-Cycle Higher Education - A Search for Identity, OECD, Paris, 1973.
2.   Cf. Study I in "Towards Mass Higher Education ...", op. cit.
3.   Other, more fundamental factors also play a role, particularly the social values reflected in the choice of study, and they will be examined in later sections of this paper.
4.   The high drop-out rates from universities (up to 60% before the end of the second year) indicates that there is a potential for the development of short-cycle studies.

The first of these solutions was adopted by several European countries during the sixties, e. g. the creation of two-year institutions such as the Norwegian Regional Colleges, the French University Institutes of Technology (IUTs), and the Yugoslav Više Škole. (1)   Adoption of the second solution seems to have been increasingly advocated in the early seventies, as reflected in the most recent proposals in the United Kingdom and France to create a two-year polyvalent degree (Higher Education Diploma and the Diplôme d'études universitaires générales). The third, most radical solution, which was adopted by the universities of Roskilde (Denmark), Bremen (Germany) and a few others, (2) relates to the whole philosophy and principles inherent in the concept of recurrent education.

The available data do not provide a clear picture of the prevailing trends in the different modes of study and attendance. In general, the proportion of those enrolled in part-time studies remained relatively stable during the sixties; in the case of the United Kingdom there was a marked decrease while in Canada the proportion increased. Whether the fact that there has been no massive expansion of part-time studies (or of sandwich and evening courses) is due to a lack of facilities for these studies, or to the continued prestige and attractiveness of traditional patterns, remains an open question which obviously has important policy implications.

The diversification of patterns of study and modes of attendance is clearly reflected in the recent trend towards the development of the so-called "non-traditional" patterns of study. (3)   These are essentially "age-free", "time-free" and "space-free" patterns of education, that is patterns not closely linked to specific age periods, fixed durations or particular geographic locations. The first consequence of such a system will almost inevitably be a blurring of the line which until now has separated the education of young people from that of adults, which is clearly a prerequisite to bridging the generation gap and to the development of a recurrent education system. It will also provide the necessary flexibility between educational opportunities and work experience which will be of benefit to both higher education institutions and the employment situation.

d)   Institutions

It should be clear by now that diversification of access routes, of curricula, of modes of attendance, etc. , can take place through both a multiplicity of institutions or categories of institutions, and within one dominant institutional type. This is the substance of the whole debate between the protagonists of the comprehensive university model and those who defend various forms of binary or, more precisely, "multi-institutional" model. Neither of the two alternatives can be said to be inherently better than the other. Optimum solutions will depend on the national context and traditions, and especially on the capacity and willingness of the universities to assume an internal diversification.

1.   The problems of these institutions were examined by the Secretariat in its previous work on short-cycle higher education: See Short-Cycle Higher Education - A Search for Identity, op. cit.

2.   See Study III "The Integration of Learning and Research in Mass Higher Education: Towards a New Concept of Science" in Structure of Studies ..., op. cit.

3.   See "New Approaches in Post-Secondary Education", op. cit., and section II of the "Guidelines for Discussion", Part Two of the present volume.

In other words it can be said that the majority of countries are faced with the choice of either radically reforming their existing university sector by providing within it the new mass higher education facilities outlined above, or concentrating these facilities in a parallel sector whose links with the former will be progressively strengthened. A clear example of this latter case is the United Kingdom binary system where although links between the two sectors remain for the moment very weak, the non-university sector comprises all the levels of study from sub-degree to doctorate. In practice, however, mixed solutions are frequently adopted which give different emphasis to one or other of the two alternatives.

This leads to the identification of four models:(1)

i) the integrated comprehensive university model, (e. g. the German "Gesamthochschule" and the Danish University Centre projects);

ii) the binary model (the United Kingdom and to some extent Ontario in Canada);

iii) the combined development model (e. g. Norway, emphasizing the development of a new network of Regional Colleges and a partial reform of universities with close links between the two; France with its radical reform of universities and the creation and development of IUTs; Yugoslavia, Belgium and to some extent the United States);

iv) the first-cycle multi-purpose college model (e. g. "Collèges d'enseignement général et professionnel" in Quebec, and partly in the United States).

Recent developments in Member countries do not allow conclusions to be drawn on whether any one of these four models is becoming predominant. The comprehensive university model is the object of several experimental undertakings (Roskilde, Bremen, Loughborough in England and, to a certain extent, the Extended University Program of the University of California). (2) At the same time, Germany, which envisaged making the integrated comprehensive university the basic organisational unit of its higher education system, seems to be retreating towards a rather loose version of this model (Co-operative "Gesamthochschule"), while other countries are definitely introducing their most innovative experiences outside the established universities.

Thus the choice of strategies for diversification will to a large extent depend on the attitude of, and role assigned to, the universities. If new and non-traditional forms of education are accepted as an integral part of the internal organisation and of the goal and value structure of universities, and there is a willingness to accept a diversified student population of both youth and adults, the comprehensive university model would probably represent the optimum solution. If, on the other hand, universities adhere strictly to their traditional patterns, functions and standards, there will be no alternative but to develop new types of institutions to assume the new forms of post-secondary education.

In practice, of course, universities although often fully autonomous are everywhere subject to increased governmental pressure motivated by both financial considerations and manpower and other socio-economic

1. Cf. "Towards New Structures of Post-Secondary Education", op. cit., pp. 38-39.

2. Cf. "A Strategy for Change in Higher Education: The Extended University of the University of California", op. cit.

and political preoccupations. These pressures will almost certainly lead to new attitudes on the part of the universities and, consequently, in many cases intermediary solutions will have to be found.

3. DILEMMAS OF DIVERSIFICATION

a) Rigid versus flexible structures

The above discussion shows that the essential characteristic of a diversified post-secondary system is the existence of alternatives, that is the availability of multiple possibilities of entry into the system and of what, how and where to study. This principle also applies to areas which have not been discussed in this paper, such as the degree structure, the internal organisation of institutions, the recruitment of staff, etc.: a diversified system will tend towards a wider range of degrees, towards a network of institutions with a variety of organisational units (departments, institutes, schools, etc.) and patterns of governance, and towards the recruitment of teachers with very different educational and professional backgrounds.

Such diversification by itself, however, does not guarantee that old rigidities will not be replaced by new ones and that open and flexible structures will necessarily emerge. The deep-rooted values and attitudes of the different social groups concerned give rise to a strong propensity to reinterpret almost any innovation in traditional terms. Thus, new curricula and new degrees have been established but their attraction and prestige has remained low compared to traditional ones; new access routes to post-secondary education have been opened but a "voie royale" has remained. The same danger undoubtedly confronts the most recent diversification measures: the expansion of non-traditional forms of study is encouraged but they are in danger of remaining the "less noble" sector in terms of career possibilities, quality of teaching and status. The problem is identical to that analysed by the Secretariat in connection with its work on short-cycle higher education. (1) Surveys on the student population in three new types of non-university institution have shown that these populations include a large proportion of students of middle class origin with lower educational qualifications than those of their university counterparts; and a minority of students - although larger than that in the universities - from the lower classes with high education standards. (2) This can be considered as a positive development towards democratization but, at the same time, it strengthens the "less noble" image of these institutions.

The potential or actual distortion of the process of diversification usually gives rise to two types of measure:

  i) The new institutions or patterns of study are given a certain number of attributes which make their image resemble slightly that of the traditional, prestigious institutions. Including the word "university" in the name of the institution, as in the French IUT's or the British Open University, is a case in point. But usually there is more than terminology involved: the standards are supposed to be as high, the degrees awarded are of the same kind, the duration of study is more or less equivalent

---

1. Cf. Short-Cycle Higher Education - A Search for Identity, op. cit.
2. For more details see "Students in University Institutes of Technology in France", OECD Document, Paris, 1973.

44

to those in universities. This approach could perhaps be labelled as an attempt to generalize elite higher education. The danger which this approach implies is obvious: by trying to resemble the traditional "noble" model of higher education the new schemes might rapidly lose the very purpose for which they were created. The diversification process becomes, in fact, a process of segmentation (1) - and the need for diversification subsists with all the tensions which this need, if unfulfilled, generates.

ii) Devices and mechanisms are provided which closely link the old and the new patterns. This implies in particular the creation of transfer possibilities for students (as well as for teachers) between the traditional and non-traditional forms of study. This is dealt with in the following section.

The most important obstacle to "de-hierarchization" lies probably in the prevailing differences in the working conditions and reward structures for teachers in different institutions as well as in the market value of their graduates. These are not easy to overcome because they reflect long-established value structures in society which view the educational system as a selection/certification mechanism for the professions. There will of course always be some teachers and institutions which are better than others, learning situations which are more successful than others. The important point is that these unavoidable differences should not be reflected in one single, rigid hierarchy but in a plurality of hierarchies. In other words, the system should not be dominated by a "unidimensional criterion of evaluation"(2) which automatically creates a pressure for uniformity that works against diversity. The ability of a diversification process to avoid this danger will depend to a large extent on the possibilities for change within the existing value structure. This will be examined later.

b) Transferability

It is certain that transferability is one of the key features of a flexible and diversified structure of post-secondary education; however, recent experiences show that the implementation of such a principle poses a number of problems that have no easy solutions. Transferability exists when the component parts of the system are organised and interrelate in such a way that students (or teachers) may transfer from one institution or educational scheme to another at minimum cost. Clearly, the most ambitious concepts in this respect are to be found in the comprehensive universities, such as the University Centre (Denmark) and the California Plan. But transferability can also be envisaged between patterns and institutions which keep their own administrative or legal identity. Conversely, a hierarchical structure with only insignificant flows and mobility between its components can also exist within a comprehensive institution.

Absolute transferability is obviously impossible, but certainly the curriculum content of related fields of study (health, technical, social studies) can be made more polyvalent to avoid the old dichotomy between

---

1. Segmentation can be defined as a process "in which two or more structurally distinct roles or collectivities perform essentially the same function". Robert Marsh. Comparative Sociology, op.cit., p. 31.

2. A.G. Watts, Diversity and Choice in Higher Education, Routledge and Kegan Paul, London, 1972, p. 40.

practical or vocational and theoretical or academic education. This polyvalence has its limits, but these could surely be determined in a more liberal and flexible way. (1) The second limit to transferability derives from the fact that some of the conditions necessary to achieve it perfectly could easily distort the diversification process and thus risk giving the system an undesirable uniformity. If, for example, most of the entrants to short-cycle institutions expect to transfer to university, and if these institutions agree to fulfil this role, they risk becoming mere antechambers of universities, neglecting their specific functions and simply abiding by the rules of the senior institutions. On the other hand, if the possibilities of pursuing further studies are totally restricted, short-cycle institutions will be perceived as blind alleys and not as acceptable alternatives to long-cycle studies. The search for equivalence, and not for equality, will thus be one of the major challenges for new post-secondary institutions.

c) "Diversification" of values

Curiously enough, the existing value structure, which places the highest value on theoretically and academically oriented higher education and on involvement in pure research, and the lowest value on work-related or vocationally-centred training, is as much contested in "progressive" circles as any other characteristic of present-day industrial societies. The quest for relevance, the need for a service function for higher education and for its closer integration into society are universal. Yet, in actual fact, it is the process of diversifying values which is probably the least advanced. Diversity becomes hierarchy, and new rigidities emerge for this more than any other reason. A number of examples can be quoted: students who resist the introduction of new degrees because they do not correspond to the standard norm; governments who create new patterns of study but do not give them recognition in their civil service scales; employers who criticize the abstract nature of university education but recruit more university graduates than graduates of non-traditional streams; trade unions who fight for equality of opportunity but see it only in the framework of an extension of the elite university; professional associations who complain about the out-dated nature of existing university education but who, through their influence over the certification process, often block the really innovative solutions. The list could be made much longer and more specific.

The most critical consequence of this situation seems to be in the relations between education and employment. It is here that the contradictions are most obvious between the nature and functions of mass higher education and the values of the social groups concerned. Unemployment of graduates, inadaptation of educational qualifications to job requirements, mismatch between the output of the education system and the needs of the economy - these all surely pose important problems for present higher education systems and for society at large. (2) But, they are usually completely misunderstood because they are still interpreted in

1. In fact, society itself often adopts a more liberal attitude. In some countries up to 50% of graduates in engineering do not work as engineers, and up to 50% of those assuming professional engineer functions are not graduates of engineering schools. Similarly, a large proportion of law graduates never take up a legal profession. There is no reason why the rules of the education system should be so much more rigid than those of society.

2. Cf. Study III "New Relations between Post-Secondary Education and Employment" in "Towards Mass Higher Education ...", op. cit.

the same way as they were when only 4 to 6% of the age group benefited from higher education, which is clearly inappropriate in a situation where this proportion is over 20%. To the extent that the expectations of students, teachers, parents and other social groups with regard to mass higher education remain the same as they were under conditions of elite higher education, it will be difficult to arrive at viable solutions.

It is true that, contrary to what was the case in the fifties and early sixties, and in spite of rapid technological progress, requirements for high-level manpower have grown less rapidly than enrolments in higher education.(1) The tension generated by the resulting imbalance is sharpened because of the persistence of exclusive elite attitudes and values. It is, in other words, a cultural as much as an economic pheno-menon. The imbalance or mismatch is as much between the product of higher education and the needs of society as it is between those needs and society's expectations of higher education. Rejecting the selection process for entry into post-secondary education and allowing students a free choice of studies are clearly in fundamental contradiction with grad-uates' expectations of employment in privileged positions.

Since the late sixties, however, there have been clear indications that new sets of values are emerging which have an impact on higher education: the growing reaction against economic growth per se, different aspects of the student counter-culture, the deschooling concepts, a cer-tain disenchantment with science, etc. , are undoubtedly signs of a more pluralistic value structure penetrating the new world of learning.

Clearly, the present system of higher education is by no means the only cause of this "uni-dimensionality" and of the prevailing rigid value structure which blocks so many innovations. But it is nonetheless responsible in large part, especially the universities which by the content of their teaching contribute greatly to the impression that all their stu-dents will end up in elite positions. By giving so much weight and prestige to theory over practice, to fundamental over applied research, they in-evitably lead many people to believe that their training is essentially destined for the privileged. This raises the question of how higher edu-cation can help to change the value structure and (more relevant to the context of the present paper) which structural changes are necessary to help attain a system of multi-dimensional or pluralistic values.

For obvious reasons, only a summary answer to this question can be attempted here. Reforms in the field of curriculum and structure of studies as examined above are certainly one of the first requirements. Blurring the line which at present separates theoretical and academic from practical and vocational courses is particularly important and might best be achieved by a quasi-mandatory mix of these two types of education in all sectors, at all stages and levels of post-secondary education. An-other powerful device would be a radical transformation of the reward system for both teachers and students and of the criteria governing sal-aries, promotion, evaluation of achievement, award of degrees, trans-fers, etc. A third category of measures relates to budgetary incentives which can relatively easily be oriented towards particular objectives connected with new values.

Many of these measures are being tried out in different Member countries but they do not appear to be used in a systematic way, in other words they are not implemented as a coherent whole. There is in parti-cular a lack of sustained effort in their application, for instance there is no continuous evaluation of their positive effects, weaknesses and dis-tortions.

This leads to some concluding remarks concerning the actual pro-cess of structural transformation and the problem of overcoming the resistances and constraints which might prevent or slow down this process.

1. Ibid.

CONCLUSION: STRATEGIES FOR STRUCTURAL CHANGE

One general conclusion which emerges from the above analysis is that desirable changes towards a more open, flexible and diversified system of higher education will not come about spontaneously. They will need to be supported by a planning process not the least aim of which should be to encourage the creation of a system of incentives, rewards and other devices necessary to promote the acceptance of change in the face of established values and social inertia.

Two, almost contradictory requirements have to be reconciled, namely those arising from the postulate of diversity, with all that this implies in terms of autonomy, and those involved in traditional concepts of the planning process, which implies co-ordination and even a certain degree of centralization. This dichotomy is also reflected in the essential characteristics of new structures of post-secondary education, that is their unity and diversity, unity implying "effective co-ordination of the various existing institutions as well as a minimum of integrated planning". (1)

A second, and related conclusion points to the need for a comprehensive strategy for the planning of future structures of post-secondary education. It must be comprehensive in two senses: on the one hand, it is essential that it be concerned with the total sector of educational activity that society provides beyond the compulsory school level, whether within the formal system or outside it; on the other hand, no development strategy can afford to address itself to single issues or groups of issues in isolation because of the inextricable links which have been shown to exist between the goals of the system, numbers, costs, structural and pedagogical changes, and economic and broader social considerations. Behind these considerations lies the growing realization of the interdependency of higher education policies and public policies in other sectors, and of the consequent need for such policies to be closely co-ordinated if the new social objectives that governments are setting themselves for the seventies are to be effectively pursued.

In practice, both the above conclusions lead to the recognition that more attention should be paid to planning not only the means of bringing about structural transformation but also the ways of overcoming resistance to the planned objectives while at the same time mobilizing their political and social support. It is in this sense that widespread involvement in planning and implementing the directions of change as is implied in the concept of "participation" becomes a practical necessity and the major task now confronting the planning of post-secondary education. The goals of future structures of post-secondary education cannot in fact be separated, conceptually or in practice, from the process by which

---

1. See "Towards New Structures of Post-Secondary Education", op. cit., p. 32.

48

they are formulated, or from the process and means by which the desired structural changes are to be achieved.

The analysis suggests that the implementation of such strategies for change comes up against a set of major constraints in terms of costs, the employment situation, and the political, historical and sociological context.

With regard to costs, probably one of the key questions is whether non-traditional forms of post-secondary education can, in purely financial terms, bring about any significant reductions in unit costs. A priori, this seems to be the case for schemes such as the Open University or the Empire State College; but the danger here is that for precisely this reason such schemes might also be considered as "cheap" higher education in the qualitative sense and consequently be accepted by society as only second best. In the last analysis, reductions in costs will depend on political decisions as to what can be given up in the present functioning of the system, and this is not really amenable to scientific analysis.

With regard to the constraints imposed upon education by the real or assumed needs of the labour market, it has been argued above that whatever might be the mismatch between the output of post-secondary education and manpower requirements, solutions must be sought on the basis of an appreciation of the new, much more diffuse relations that exist between education and employment in a mass system which is markedly different from that of the past. It is obviously essential that everyone concerned be fully aware of this. Employers (including the administration, which should perhaps play a leading role here) will need to develop more flexible recruitment practices, free of rigid scales classifying each individual according to the kind of degree received. Higher education programmes will have to undergo greater "professionalization" through a more flexible combination of theoretical and vocational courses at all levels. Teachers and institutions of post-secondary education must evolve more effective guidance and orientation functions which take into account the new, diffuse relations between education and employment and, of course, bring this to bear on their curricula. Education and employment authorities will need to co-operate more closely to establish more flexible relations between education and professional experience so that learning opportunities can be spread over a longer period in the life-span of the individual, and these in turn could be combined into more flexible patterns of career development. Above all, the students themselves and their unions must become conscious of the new situation and accept it not as a shortcoming of the system or as a temporary phenomenon but as a structural feature of mass higher education to which they must adjust their aspirations and scale of values.

Finally, the search for new structures in higher education will of course need to build on and reflect the politico-historical and sociological contexts which are peculiar to each country. The danger here is that the argument of incompatibility with national traditions may be all too easily invoked to resist changes based on "foreign" models. The assumptions behind much of the argument in the present report have been that through a functional analysis of the different models being developed in Member countries useful insights might be obtained into the options open to these countries in their search for their own solutions to the fundamental issues confronting all higher education systems. (1) In the last analysis, how-

1. Thus, for example, it is probable that the different types of community colleges as they developed in the United States and Canada cannot and should not be duplicated in Europe. But the functions which they assume, and to a great extent the problems which they have to face in the existing mass post-secondary education systems of North America, must certainly be assumed and faced in the emerging mass systems of Europe; in other words, appropriate functional substitutes have to be found.

ever, such solutions will not be effective unless seen as part of the general process of social change. This means that provision for bringing about changes in the behaviour and attitudes of social groups concerned, as a prerequisite to the acceptance of change, must be effectively built into any strategy for structural reform in post-secondary education.

In other words, it is not sufficient to postulate more autonomy, more interdisciplinarity, more diversification, more equality of opportunity; it is not even sufficient to provide the necessary means to attain these objectives unless at the same time ways are proposed (and implemented) by which people and institutions actually will assume more autonomy, will accept the interdisciplinary approach, will interpret and respond to the requirements of diversification and equality of opportunity in their comprehensive and pluralistic sense.

III

PROBLEMS IN THE TRANSITION FROM ELITE TO MASS HIGHER EDUCATION

by

Martin Trow

University of California, Berkeley
United States

CONTENTS

INTRODUCTION

In every advanced society the problems of higher education are problems associated with growth. Growth poses a variety of problems for the educational systems that experience it and the societies which support them. These problems arise in every part of higher education - in its finance, its government and administration; in its recruitment and selection of students; in its curriculum and forms of instruction; in its recruitment, training and socialization of staff; in the setting and maintenance of standards; in the forms of examinations and the nature of qualifications awarded; in student housing and job placement; in motivation and morale; in the relation of research to teaching; in the relation of higher education to the secondary school system on one hand and to adult education on the other - growth has its impact on every form of activity and manifestation of higher education.

In most of the writing on higher education in recent years these problems are treated in isolation. Discussions of curriculum reform are commonly carried on quite separately from discussions of finance and administration, by different people with different methods and assumptions and often different values; they are reported in different conferences and published in different journals for different audiences. Similarly, discussions of student unrest and disruptions in the universities more often make reference to student politics and ideology than to the changing relation of higher education to the occupational structures of advanced industrial societies. This paper will argue that these problems can be understood better as different manifestations of a related cluster of problems arising out of the transition from one phase to another in a broad pattern of development of higher education that is under way in every advanced society: from elite to mass higher education and subsequently towards universal access. Underlying this pattern of development lies growth and expansion.

ASPECTS OF GROWTH

The growth of higher education manifests itself in at least three quite different ways, and these in turn give rise to different sets of problems. There is first the rate of growth - and in many Western European countries the number of students in higher education doubled within five-year periods during the sixties and will have doubled again in seven, eight or ten years by the mid-seventies. Growth obviously affects the absolute size of both systems and individual institutions. Third, growth is reflected in changes in the proportion of the relevant age grade enrolled in higher education institutions.

Each of these manifestations of growth carries its own peculiar problems in its train. For example, a high growth rate places great strains on the existing structures of governance, administration and, above all, of socialization. When a very large proportion of all the members of an institution are new recruits, they threaten to overwhelm the processes whereby recruits to a more slowly growing system are inducted into its value system and learn its norms and forms. When a faculty or department grows from, say, five to twenty members within three or four years, and when the new staff are predominantly young men and women fresh from post-graduate study, then they largely define the norms of academic life in that faculty and its standards. If the post-graduate student population also grows rapidly and there is loss of a close apprenticeship relationship between faculty members and students, then the student culture becomes the chief socializing force for new post-graduate students, with the consequences for the intellectual and academic life of the institution that we have seen in America as well as in France, Italy, West Germany and Japan. High growth rates increase the chances for academic innovation; they also weaken the forms and processes by which teachers and students are inducted into a community of scholars during periods of stability or slow growth.

Absolute size has a variety of consequences for academic life. Growth may take the form of very large institutions, or of a very large system, or of both. When growth results in large institutions it has effects on the nature of the milieux in which teaching, learning and research go on. Large size affects the norms as well as the structures of higher education. For example, there is an academic norm, quite appropriate to the relatively small institutions of elite higher education, which prescribes that an academic man has an obligation to be of help with his time, advice and so forth, to anyone in any discipline in his own university and to anyone anywhere in the world in his own discipline. During the last two decades in every advanced country in the world the numbers in almost every discipline have grown very substantially, while many institutions have doubled, tripled or quadrupled their size. The norms of academic life have not significantly changed over this time. And this gives rise to what might be called a pattern of "institutionalized distraction". Academic men of middle and senior rank find that the number of requests for demands on their time and attention increases at least in proportion to the growth in the numbers of "relevant colleagues", and probably much faster given the patterns of communication in scholarly life. The whole level of pace and activity increases: men are invited to consult on other people's projects, to go to increasing numbers of conferences, to referee more papers for more journals, and to carry the much more complex burdens of administration that are associated with large institutions and systems.

It becomes increasingly difficult for academic men to protect the uninterrupted time that they need for fresh thinking about their subjects or for carrying on their scholarly work and research. This is a price paid for growth that is rarely taken into account by students of the costs and benefits of higher education. In response to increased demands on people's time, academic men begin to devise patterns of evasion: men spend less time in their offices and more at home; they are more likely to take research leave away from their institutions; they rely more on their research institutes and centres. These centrifugal forces in turn tend to weaken the academic communities which have sustained the norms of academic life, with very marked consequences for both the governance of universities and the training and socialization of students, both under-graduate and graduate.

Growth affects the size of the national system as well as its component units, and here the effects are primarily economic and political. As a system grows it emerges from the obscurity of the relatively small elite system with its comparatively modest demands on national resources and becomes an increasingly substantial competitor for public expenditures along with housing, welfare and defence. As it does so, higher education comes increasingly to the attention of larger numbers of people, both in government and in the general public, who have other, often quite legitimate, ideas about where public funds should be spent and, if given to higher education, how they should be spent. The relation of higher education to the state becomes more and more critical the bigger the system of higher education, and this is especially true in most European countries where the state and local government are almost the sole source of funds for higher education. Under these conditions the questions of academic freedom and institutional autonomy become central political questions and not something to be arranged, as formerly, by a few old friends in the universities and in the ministries of education and finance who share very similar views of the world and who may well have attended the elite universities together. Growth raises the question of the relation of the state to higher education in new and disturbing ways.

Growth also manifests itself in the growing proportions of the age grade in any society enrolled in institutions of higher education. In many European countries just after World War II, that proportion was about 4 or 5%. Now, only 25 years later, it is between 10 and 15% in a range of Western European countries, with a few exceeding the upper figure. Growth in the proportions of the population that have access to higher education raises a number of questions central to the issue of mass higher education. For example, in every country, the proportions entering higher education vary very sharply between different regional groups, religious and ethnic groups and socio-economic classes. The proportions from the upper and middle classes are everywhere significantly higher than those from the working classes or farmers. When the proportions of an age grade going into higher education were very small, the political issue of equality of educational opportunity was centred much more on higher primary and secondary education. But the higher the proportion of the age grade going on to higher education, the more the democratic and egalitarian concerns for equality of opportunity come to centre on the increasingly important sector of tertiary education. These differences in access to higher education, which are not reduced but rather increased during the early stages of expansion, become a sharp political issue in the context of democratic and egalitarian values and create strong pressures for reducing these differences in group rates of enrolment. The more important entry to higher education is for the life chances of large numbers of students, the stronger these pressures become. The persistent tendency of intellectually elite institutions such as the universities to be also the home of the social and economic elite is a major source of tension between the institutions of higher education and the increasingly strong egalitarian values of Western society.

The rising rate of enrolment of an age grade has another important significance, one not so directly political. As more students from an age cohort go to college or university each year, the meaning of college attendance changes - first from being a privilege to being a right, and then, as is increasingly true in the United States, to being almost an obligation. This shift in the meaning and significance of attendance in the tertiary sector has enormous consequences for student motivation, and thus also for the curriculum and for the intellectual climate of these institutions. This question will be discussed later in the paper.

PHASES IN THE DEVELOPMENT OF HIGHER EDUCATION

There is no question about the extent and speed of expansion of European higher education; indeed, that story has been documented in great detail in recent OECD publications. (1) For example, Sweden had 14,000 university students in 1947. By 1960 the number had more than doubled to 35,000; by 1965 it had doubled again to about 70,000, with another doubling by 1971, when university students comprised about 24% of the relevant age group. France saw a growth in its university population between 1960 and 1965 of from 200,000 to over 400,000, with another doubling by the mid-seventies projected to an enrolment rate of about 17% of the age group. Denmark doubled its university student population between 1960 and 1966 from 19,000 to 34,000; by the mid-seventies it will double again by 70,000 at which time the university student population will comprise about 13% of the age group. In the United Kingdom the Robbins Report anticipated university enrolments growing from about 130,000 in 1962 to 220,000 by 1973 and to nearly 350,000 by 1980. These projections have already been substantially revised upwards towards 400,000 (about 13% of the age group) in all forms of full-time higher education by 1973, and somewhere between 800,000 and 1,000,000 by 1981, with roughly half in universities.

What these numbers conceal are two fundamentally different processes. One of these is the expansion of the elite universities - the growth of traditional university functions in traditional, if somewhat modified, forms of universities. The other is the transformation of elite university systems into systems of mass higher education performing a great variety of new functions (at least new to universities) for a much larger proportion of the university age group. Up to the present in Britain, as on the continent, growth has mainly been achieved by expanding the elite university system. But the institutions cannot expand indefinitely; they are limited by their traditions, organisation, functions and finance. In European countries it is likely that an increased enrolment in higher education beyond about 15% of the age grade requires not merely the further expansion of the elite university systems but the rapid development of mass higher education through the growth of popular non-elite institutions. Mass higher education differs from elite higher education not only quantitatively but qualitatively. They differ obviously in the proportions of the age grade that they enrol, but also in the ways in which students and teachers view attendance in university or college; in the functions of gaining entry for the student; in the functions of the system for the society; in the curriculum; in the typical student's career; in the degree of student homogeneity; in the character of academic standards; in the size of institutions; in the forms of instruction; in the relationships

1. Cf. Development of Higher Education 1950-1967: Statistical Survey, OECD, Paris, 1970.

between students and faculty; in the nature of institutional boundaries; in the patterns of institutional administration and governance; and in the principles and procedures for selecting both students and staff. In other words, the differences between these phases are quite fundamental and pervade every aspect of higher education. Let us look a little more closely at each of these aspects of higher education in its various phases.

ASPECTS OF TRANSITION

1. SIZE OF THE SYSTEM

Countries that develop a system of elite higher education in modern times seem able to expand it without changing its character in fundamental ways until it is providing places for about 15% of the age grade. At about that point the system begins to change its character; if the transition is made successfully the system is then able to develop institutions that can grow without being transformed until they reach about 50% of the age grade. Beyond that, and so far only in the United States, large sections of the population send nearly all their children to some kind of higher education, and the system must again create new forms of higher education as it begins to move rapidly toward universal access.

2. ATTITUDES TOWARD ACCESS

The ease of access to higher education is closely linked to the conceptions that people - students and their parents, and, increasingly, college and university teachers and administrators - have of college and university attendance. When access is highly limited it is generally seen as a privilege, either of birth or talent or both. When over 15% of the age grade have access, people increasingly begin to view entry to higher education as a right for those who have certain formal qualifications. When the proportion of the whole population rises to about 50% (and in certain sectors of the society it is then of course much higher) attendance in higher education is seen more and more as an obligation. For children from the middle and upper middle classes, not only in the United States but also today in European countries, not to go on to higher education from secondary school is increasingly regarded as a mark of some defect of mind or character which has to be explained or justified or apologized for. Moreover, as more people go on to higher education, the best jobs and opportunities and the economic rewards in life come to be reserved for people who have completed a university degree, and this greatly contributes to the sense of obligation that is felt by many students on entry.

3. FUNCTIONS OF HIGHER EDUCATION

The different phases are also associated with different functions of higher education both for students and for society at large. Elite higher education is concerned primarily with shaping the mind and character of the ruling class as it prepares students for broad elite roles in government and the learned professions. In mass higher education the institutions are still preparing elites, but a much broader range of elites which includes the leading strata of all the technical and economic organisations of the society. And the emphasis shifts from the shaping of character to the transmission of skills for more specific technical elite roles. In institutions marked by universal access there is for the first time concern with preparing large numbers of people for life in advanced industrial society. They are training not primarily elites, either broad or narrow, but the whole population, and their chief concern is to maximize the adaptability of that population to a society whose chief characteristic is rapid social and technological change.

4. THE CURRICULUM AND FORMS OF INSTRUCTION

The curriculum and forms of instruction naturally reflect changes in the definition of the meaning of being a student and of the functions that higher education performs for students and for the society at large. The curriculum in elite institutions has tended to be highly structured reflecting academic conceptions of the degree course or professional conceptions of professional requirements. The courses of study, shaped largely by the character of the final examination, were on the whole highly specialized and governed by the professors' notions of what constituted an educated man or a qualified professional. In institutions of mass higher education, education becomes more modular, marked by semi-structured sequences of courses, which increasingly earn unit credits (the unit of exchange in modular courses), allowing more flexible combinations of course and easier access and movement between major fields and, indeed, among institutions. (1) In universal higher education, as it emerges, there is a survival of the modular course but instruction is becoming relatively less structured; the boundaries of the course itself begin to break down, as do required sequences of courses. It is very difficult to justify course requirements where no single conception of higher education is accepted, and the rejection of academic forms, structures and standards also extends to examinations and assessment as distinctions between learning and life become attenuated. Attendance at the emerging higher education institutions designed for universal access is merely another kind of experience, not qualitatively different from any other experiences in modern society which give one resources for coping with the problems of contemporary life. And, in a universal access system, since course work does not clearly qualify people for specific jobs, it is less clear why assessment of performance is necessary.

There are parallel differences in the typical forms of instruction and thus in the relationships between student and teacher. In elite systems the characteristic form of instruction is the tutorial or seminar, marked on the whole by a personal relationship between student and teacher. (2) This is compatible with the central function of the shaping of

1. Unit credits and a modular curriculum are much more common in higher technical colleges than in European universities.

2. While the distance between the senior professor and the ordinary undergraduate may be very great, his research students are likely to be working with him in a close apprentice relationship.

character and the preparation of a broad or general elite whose specific adult roles and activities would vary widely making it hardly possible to train for them during the course of a university career. The defence of these forms of instruction in the "higher schools" of France during the period of rapid expansion which filled the lecture rooms of the universities to overflowing made it clear where the elite functions in France are meant to survive. Under the conditions of mass higher education the emphasis is on the transmission of skill and knowledge, and formal instruction is increasingly carried on through large lectures supplemented by seminars often taught by teaching assistants. In "universal" higher education the direct personal relationship of the student and teacher is subordinated to a broad exposure of the student to new or more sophisticated perspectives. There is heavier reliance on correspondence, use of video cassettes, TVs, computer and other technological aids to instruction.

5. THE STUDENT "CAREER"

The academic career of the student also differs. In elite institutions the student ordinarily enters directly after completion of secondary schooling; the student is "in residence" and continues his work uninterruptedly (except for holidays) until he gains a degree. He is in this sense "sponsored" and in competition only for academic honours. In the mass institution students for the most part also attend immediately after finishing secondary school, although growing numbers delay entry until after a period of work or travel. Easier access and a more heterogeneous student population lead to higher "wastage rates". But the student population is becoming a mixed residential-commuting one as vocational training becomes a larger component of higher education. In institutions of universal access there is much postponement of entry, "stopping out" (i. e. periods when the student is not in attendance), and there are large numbers of students with experience in adult occupations. The emphasis on "lifelong learning" is compatible with the softening of the boundaries between formal education and other forms of life experience.

Moreover, as student numbers grow, with increasing numbers from poor homes, a growing proportion is also working for pay in non-academic jobs - first during vacations and then during term time. This trend has implications for the meaning of being a student, for the curriculum (less outside reading and study can be assigned or assumed), for student motivations and for the relationships of students with their teachers. It is hard to discourage this practice, especially when it is done out of necessity by needy students. It can be ignored when it is the occasional "poor but able" student who has to work for his fees and maintenance. But it is a different institution when the proportion of working students is 30, 40 or 50%. The provision of state stipends for university students (as in Britain) is designed precisely to permit the maintenance of elite forms of higher education with a more "democratic" student intake. But the high and growing cost of stipends ironically acts as a brake on expansion - only one of the ways in which the principle of equality in higher education is at odds with expansion. The growing interest in student loans in several countries is part of the effort to solve this dilemma in ways that will protect the university against outside part-time work by students. The "sandwich course" for technical and vocational students is another "solution" which makes a virtue of necessity by incorporating paid work into the regular curriculum.

6. INSTITUTIONAL DIVERSITY, CHARACTERISTICS AND BOUNDARIES

Systems at different phases of their development differ also in their diversity. Elite systems tend to be highly homogeneous, the component institutions very much alike. They tend to be universities with high and common standards, though they may include highly specialized "technical schools" with special access to parts of the civil service. Mass systems begin to be more "comprehensive" with more diverse standards, though with some linkages among the several segments of the system which allow mobility of students and staff. In systems of universal access there is very great diversity in the character of component institutions, with no common standards among them. Indeed the very notion of standards is itself challenged and problematical.

The typical institutions in the three systems also differ in size and character. Elite institutions are commonly "communities" which range up to two or three thousand students in residence. If larger than three thousand they are substructured so that their component units, such as the Oxford and Cambridge colleges, tend to be relatively small. The comprehensive institutions that characterize mass higher education are less communities than they are "cities of intellect" with up to thirty or forty thousand students and staff making up a mixed residential and commuting population. Institutions of universal access are unlimited in size: they may be simply aggregates of people enrolled for "instruction", most of whom are rarely or never on the central campus; they may share little in common and do not in any sense comprise a community rooted in frequent association, shared norms and values and a sense of common identification.

As one might guess from the foregoing, elite institutions are very sharply marked off from the surrounding society by clear and relatively impermeable boundaries, in the extreme case by physical walls. In mass institutions there are still boundaries but they are more blurred and more permeable; there is relatively easy movement in and out of mass institutions and a much less clear concept of "membership", though there are still formal definitions of membership which are relevant for a variety of academic and non-academic purposes. In institutions of universal access boundaries are very weak, shading off to none at all. At a certain point anyone who may switch on a televised broadcast of a lecture may be thought of for that moment as being part of an "extended university", and the question of whether he is submitting work regularly or has matriculated is of only marginal significance. (1)

7. THE LOCUS OF POWER AND DECISION-MAKING

The three types of systems differ in their sources of ultimate authority, the nature of their academic standards, and in their principles of re-

---

1. It should not be thought that the Open University in England, despite its name, is a typical institution of universal access. On the contrary, it is a characteristically ingenious way of increasing access to an elite institution by substituting motivation for formal qualifications, and by allowing people to combine university work with full-time employment. Some of the characteristics of an elite university have been discarded, but the University maintains the high standards of elite British universities and their very clear boundaries. The Open University is an interesting transitional institution between the elite and mass phases of British higher education.

cruitment and selection. With respect to both ultimate power and effective decisions, elite institutions are dominated by relatively small elite groups: leaders in significant institutions, political, economic and academic, who know one another, share basic values and assumptions and make decisions through informal face to face contact. An example of this would be the small number of leading civil servants, government ministers, university vice-chancellors, and members of the University Grants Commission who shaped the fate of the British university system for many years in small committee rooms or around tables at the Athenaeum Club. Mass higher education continues to be influenced by these elite groups but is increasingly shaped by more "democratic" political processes and influenced by "attentive audiences". These are parts of the general public who have special interests and qualifications and who develop a common view about higher education in general or some special aspect, such as the forms and content of technical education.

Higher education policies become increasingly subject to the ordinary political processes of interest groups and party programmes. One kind of attentive audience is the employers of the products of mass higher education who are interested in the nature of their skills and qualifications. Another attentive audience is the body of "old graduates" who retain an interest in the character and fortunes of their old university. These groups often develop political instrumentalities of their own, such as associations with an elected leadership, and develop lines of communication to the smaller groups in government, legislatures and the universities themselves who make the actual decisions, both day to day and long range. When the system moves towards universal access, ever larger portions of the population begin to be affected by it, either through their own past or present attendance or that of some friend or relative. In addition, the universities and colleges - what is taught there and the activities of their staff and students - come to be of general interest, they leave the pages of the serious press and magazines and are reported in the popular journals and on television. They thus attract the interest of mass publics which see themselves more and more as having a legitimate interest in what goes on in the institutions of higher education, if for no other reason than their enormous cost and obvious impact on society. And these mass publics begin to make their sentiments known, either through letters to public officials or through their votes in special or general elections.

The change in the size and character of the publics that have an interest in higher education and exert an influence on higher educational policy greatly influences the nature and content of the discussions about higher education, who takes part in them and the decisions that flow out of them. The claims of academic men to a special expertise, and of their institutions to special privileges and immunities, are increasingly questioned; much of what academic men understand by academic freedom, and the significance of the security of academic tenure for the protection of their pursuit of truth regardless of political interests or popular sentiment, all are increasingly challenged by the growing intervention of popular sentiments into these formerly elite arenas.

8. ACADEMIC STANDARDS

The implications for academic standards are equally clear: in elite systems and institutions, at least in their meritocratic phase, these are

67

likely to be broadly shared and relatively high. In the systems and institutions of mass higher education standards become variable, differing in severity and character in different parts of the system or institution, appropriately so since both system and institution have become holding companies for quite different kinds of academic enterprises. In institutions of universal access there tends to be a different criterion of achievement: not so much the achievement of some academic standard as whether there has been any "value added" by virtue of the educational experience. That is the justification of universal higher education, as it is of the non-academic forms of primary and secondary school. Obviously this changes in a fundamental way the basis for judging individual or institutional activities. (For example, if the criterion of success is "value added" it may be better to admit students who are academically very weak rather than those with a strong record since presumably it will be easier to raise the performance of those who start low than of those who are already performing well. That argument is in fact made for the principle of open access. Whatever substance it has, it does suggest how fundamental is the shift to universal access.)

9. ACCESS AND SELECTION

The principles of student selection also vary in the different phases. In elite systems the criterion of ascribed status has given way more or less rapidly over the past century to meritocratic achievement measured by secondary school performance or grades on special examinations. In institutions of mass higher education there is a general acceptance of meritocratic criteria where access is limited, but this is qualified by a commitment to equality of educational opportunity, leading to "compensatory programmes" and the introduction of additional non-academic criteria designed to reduce "inequities" in the opportunities for admission of deprived social groups and categories. In the institutions of universal higher education, which by definition are wholly "open" to anyone who wishes to join or to those who have certain minimal educational qualifications, the criterion is whether an individual has chosen to associate himself with the institution voluntarily. The aim of universal access is towards the equality of group achievement rather than an equality of individual opportunity, and efforts are made to achieve a social, class, ethnic and racial distribution in higher education reflecting that of the population at large. Of course the more nearly the system enrols the whole of an age grade, the more closely it reflects the distribution of sub-groups in the population at large. At the limiting case, it is democratic in the same sense that compulsory forms of primary and secondary education are democratic, with surviving variations in the character and quality of the education offered in different places and different kinds of institutions. Hints of this philosophy of admissions and of these criteria for access can already be seen even in the present transitional period between mass and elite higher education in European countries.

10. FORMS OF ACADEMIC ADMINISTRATION

The characteristic institutions in the three systems differ also in their forms of institutional administration. The typical elite university is governed by part-time academics who are essentially amateurs at administration. In some countries they may have the help of a full-time civil servant or registrar to deal with routine matters or financial problems. But the head of the administrative staff is commonly an elected or appointed academic in the office for a limited period of time. As institutions become larger and their functions more varied in the phase of mass higher education, their administrative staff becomes larger; there is now more commonly a top leadership of men who were formerly academics but who now are clearly full-time university administrators. Below them there is a large and growing bureaucratic staff. As the systems grows even further towards universal access the enormous costs generate pressures for greater financial accountability and more sophisticated forms of programme management. Universities employ growing numbers of full-time professionals, such as systems analysts and economists knowledgeable in programme budgeting. The rationalization of university administration generates problems in this phase, since the functions of the institution itself have become more diverse and its "outputs" more difficult to quantify at the same time as the management procedures are becoming more dependent on quantified data for the assessment of costs and benefits.

The rationalization of university administration based on the systematic collection and analysis of quantitative data on the costs of discrete activities, and on measures of the "outputs" or "benefits" of these activities, is a response to the growth of the size and cost of higher education and to growing demands for public accountability regarding its "efficiency". But these managerial techniques, in their heavy reliance on quantified data, become a powerful independent force working against the survival of elite institutions, functions and activities which cannot be easily justified by reference to quantitative measures either of their costs or benefits. (1)

But the development of mass higher education does not necessarily involve the destruction of elite institutions or parts of institutions, or their transformation into mass institutions. Indeed, elite forms of higher education continue to perform functions that cannot be performed as well by mass higher education - among them, the education, training and socialization of very highly selected students for intellectual work at the highest standards of performance and creativity. As we observe the system of mass higher education in the United States and the patterns of growth toward mass higher education elsewhere, we see that it involves the creation and extension of functions and activities and institutions rather than the disappearance of the old.

But if elite institutions and centres tend to survive and defend their unique characteristics in the face of the growth and transformation of the system around them, they are not always successful. Their special characteristics and integrity are threatened by those egalitarian values that define all differences as inequities; by the standardizing force of central governmental control; and by the powerful levelling influence of the new

1. There is a certain danger in the argument that the development of these managerial techniques, and also of the increasing centralization of control, are "inevitable" given the growth in the size and cost of higher education. An emphasis on the inevitability of these trends and forces may preclude our asking the critical questions: how are these new administrative techniques being applied, what are their consequences, and what are the limits of centralization in relation to institutional autonomy ? We should at least be aware of how these techniques may undermine those activities and functions of higher education that cannot be justified by reference to visible and easily measurable outputs.

forms of rationalized management and administration. The rationalization of academic administration is a reflection and a product of the movement toward mass higher education; but it is not neutral toward other forms of higher education. In this respect it works against the diversity of the system that is also a characteristic - indeed, a central defining characteristic - of mass higher education. This creates a dilemma which will be discussed later in this paper.

11. INTERNAL GOVERNANCE

The forms and processes of internal governance of higher education institutions vary enormously from country to country and between institutions. But, on the whole, elite institutions everywhere tend to be governed by their senior professors;(1) those who do not hold chairs ordinarily play little or no part in major institutional decisions. As institutions, and especially their non-professorial staff, grow, the latter increasingly challenge the monopolistic power of what comes to be seen as a "professorial oligarchy". And in mass higher education, internal power comes to be shared to varying degrees with junior staff. Moreover, students increasingly claim a right to influence institutional decisions, and the forms and extent of student participation become a major issue during the transition from elite to mass higher education.

Problems of institutional governance are greatly sharpened by the breakdown of the academic consensus that occurs with growth and the transition from elite to mass higher education. Elite universities, with their narrow traditional range of functions and homogeneous bodies of students and teachers, could assume the broad acceptance by their participants of the basic character and values of the institution. But the movement toward mass higher education, with its wider range of functions, means the recruitment of new kinds of students and teachers from more diverse backgrounds and with more varied views and conceptions of what higher education and their own institutions ought to be. At the same time, junior staff, whose interests and attitudes often differ sharply from those of the senior professors, are gaining in power and influence. Students, drawn from more diverse backgrounds and affected by radical political currents, challenge many of the traditional values and assumptions of the university. In many institutions, the old consensus on which elite universities were based has broken down, both within the faculty and among the students. (2) Relations among colleagues and between teachers and students can no longer be built on a broad set of shared assumptions but are increasingly uncertain and a source of continual strain and conflict. The move toward participatory forms of governance often presupposes the survival of the old consensus, or the possibility of its recreation. But if that is an illusion (as I believe) then participatory forms of democracy may introduce into the institutions of mass higher education

1. Oxford and Cambridge, with their "aristocratic egalitarianism" among the whole body of teachers (dons), are an exception to this general rule. See A.H. Halsey and Martin Trow, The British Academics, 1971, especially Chapter 6.

2. The United States, as it moves toward universal access, is experiencing strains in the somewhat different kind of consensus on which its multiversities are based.

the conflicts of interest and ideology that are more familiar - and more easily managed - in the political institutions of society. (1)

   The politicization of the university is a familiar problem in almost all advanced societies and is the theme of much current literature. Its solution may be linked to the larger problem of devising structures that sustain educational diversity within an emerging system of mass higher education while allowing its component institutions and units to preserve their own unique identities, a narrower range of functions, and staff and students who share attitudes and values appropriate to their own institution. Consensus within units is wholly compatible with variety and diversity of forms and conceptions of higher education between units and within the larger system. But if the diversity of the whole system is reflected in each of its component units, the problems of institutional governance may become almost insoluble; in that event, as we already see in some countries, effective power and decision-making inevitably flow out of the colleges and universities into the hands of political authorities whose authority is based not on their roles in higher education but on the political processes of the larger society. The breakdown of institutional governance arising out of value dissensus and fiercely politicized conflicts of values and interests tends to weaken the autonomy of an institution: someone has to make decisions and account for public funds in ways broadly acceptable to the society at large, and if this cannot be done inside the institution then it will be done by outsiders or their appointees.

---

1.   This reference to student participation illustrates a general principle that emerges from this analysis: that the "same" phenomenon may have very different meanings and consequences in different phases of higher education. Thus "student participation" in the governance of a small, elite institution marked by high value consensus may in fact be merely the participation of the most junior members of a corporate body. By contrast, "student participation" in a large mass institution marked by value dissensus may heighten the kind of interest and ideological conflicts that academic institutions, whatever their size or character, have great difficulty in containing or resolving. This is not always recognized; and the arguments for student participation drawn from experience in elite universities are often applied indiscriminately to mass institutions. (This is also true of other aspects of governance and forms of administration.)

CAVEATS

There are several important caveats to be made before developing this perspective further.

i) First: the three phases - elite, mass and universal higher education - are, in Max Weber's sense, ideal types. They are abstracted from empirical reality, and emphasize the functional relationships among the several components of an institutional system common to all advanced industrial societies rather than the unique characteristics of any one. Therefore, the description of any phase cannot be taken as a full or adequate description of any single national system.

ii) Second: these ideal types are designed to define and illuminate the problems of higher education common to a number of countries. These problems are of three broad kinds:

- The functional relationships among the various components or aspects of given systems: for example, the degree of compatibility or strain between a given pattern of student admissions and the dominant forms of university curriculum.
- The problems arising during the transition from one phase to the next when existing, more or less functional relationships are progressively disrupted by uneven and differently timed changes in the patterns and characteristics of the system. An example might be the survival of the professorial oligarchy as a mode of institutional, faculty or departmental governance as the growth in the numbers and functions of junior staff increases their responsibilities, importance and self-confidence.
- The problems arising in the relations between institutions of higher education and the larger society and its economic and political institutions, as higher education moves from one phase to another. An example here might be the greater concern for public accountability of funds spent on higher education, and the greater interference with the autonomy of higher education institutions in the allocation and use of these funds, as costs rise and the higher education system becomes more consequential and more significant to a wider range of social, political and economic activities.

iii) Third: it must be emphasized that the movement of a system from elite to mass higher education, or from mass to universal higher education, does not necessarily mean that the forms and patterns of the prior phase or phases disappear or are transformed. On the contrary, the evidence suggests that each phase survives in some institutions and in parts of others while the system as a whole evolves to carry the larger numbers of students and the broader, more diverse functions of the next phase. Its newest and gradually its most important institutions have the characteristics of the next phase. But in a mass system elite institutions may not only survive but flourish; and elite functions may continue to be performed within mass institutions. (Similarly, both elite and mass institutions survive as the United States moves towards universal access to higher education.) But this observation points to a characteristic problem of all mixed-phase systems: the problem arising from the strains inherent in the continuing existence of forms of higher education based on fundamentally different principles and oriented to quite different kinds of functions. The question follows: how successfully, through what institutions and mechanisms, does a system continue to perform elite functions when the emphasis of the system has shifted to the forms and functions of mass higher education? How successfully can a system perform diverse functions which require quite different structures, values and relationships - especially when central governing agencies are pressed by both bureaucratic rules and egalitarian politics to treat institutions and individuals equally and in standard ways?

iv) Fourth: the analysis of the phases of development of higher education should not be taken to imply that the elements and components of a system of higher education change at equal rates, and that a system moves evenly toward the characteristic forms of the next phase. In fact, development is very uneven: numerical expansion may produce a more diversified student body before the curriculum has been similarly diversified; the curriculum may become more diversified before the recruitment and training of staff have changed to meet the new requirements of the changed curriculum; the staff may have become more diverse before the forms of institutional governance reflect the changes in the character of university and college teachers, and begin to distribute institutional authority to reflect more closely academic responsibility. A close analysis of developments in any system must attend to the sequence of change in its several parts and patterns; to the consequent strains and problems; and to the extent to which the changes in different countries show common sequential patterns among the various parts and elements of their systems.

In short, the analysis of the phases of higher education in advanced industrial societies, of the development of parts of the system during these phases, and of the problems that arise at the transition points between phases and among elements changing at different rates within a phase, is designed to illuminate problems and patterns common to different societies and systems.

74

VARIATIONS IN THE PATTERNS OF CHANGE

There are several questions that may be asked about the patterns of change in the course of the growth and transformation of higher education in advanced industrial societies.

    i) Is there a characteristic pattern in the sequence of change of higher education systems? If so, what is that pattern?

    ii) Which elements of higher education change more or less easily, and which are highly resistant to change in the course of growth?

    iii) What are the consequences of variations in the rate of change among the several elements of a system of higher education?

It is not possible to do more here than suggest tentative and provisional answers to these questions.

The expansion of student numbers seems to precede other institutional changes in almost all cases. Systems of higher education do not characteristically modify their arrangements in anticipation of growth. (Indeed the rate and amount of expansion, at least in the earlier phases of growth spurts, is commonly underestimated.) The one major exception to this was the "land grant" state universities in America after the Civil War. These institutions, already democratic and comprehensive in conception and devoted equally to scholarship, vocational studies and public service, were far ahead of their time; they were, in fact institutions dedicated to mass higher education long before college and university enrolments reached anything like the proportions which characterize mass higher education. This important development, arising more out of the egalitarian values of the United States and the role of education in its political philosophy, greatly eased the transition from elite to mass higher education in that country. Thus it is only experiencing now, in its move toward universal higher education, the problems that European countries are experiencing in their move from elite to mass higher education.

The growth of numbers, in itself, begins to change the conception that students have of their attendance in college or university. When enrolment rates are four or five per cent of the age grade, students naturally see themselves as part of a highly privileged minority; while this does not mean that they are necessarily passive or deferential, it does make them feel, along with their professors and lecturers, part of a small privileged institution with a very clear set of common interests embodied in a common life style, values, symbols and ceremonies and modes of speech. All this affirmed the communal identity of the academic institution over and against the rest of society. Students might indeed be highly rebellious, but their actions and demonstration were typically directed against state or political institutions rather than against members of their own institution.

Growth toward enrolment of 15 to 20% of the age grade, and toward student numbers in the larger European countries of half a million rather than fifty thousand, inevitably changed that. Students increasingly came to see their entry into a university as a right earned by fulfilling certain requirements. For some, and a growing proportion, attendance is in part becoming obligatory: larger numbers in all countries attend university at least partly because people in their parents' social strata send their children to university as a matter of course. Such students feel less like members of a chosen elite on arrival, and they enter universities which are larger (and in some cases very much larger) than their counterparts of twenty years ago. These big institutions are marked in many cases by impersonality, turbulence and continuing political activity. There is little question that the "communal" aspects of universities have declined along with the sense on the part of the students and teachers of their being members of a special "estate".

The growth of numbers and the shift in the conception of attendance from privilege to right is accompanied by changes in the principles and processes of selection. As the gates gradually open, the older, almost exclusive links between a handful of elite preparatory schools (whether private or state supported) and the universities become attenuated, and new avenues of access to higher education begin to open up. Logically, if the move toward mass higher education were state policy and carefully planned, the development of a broad system of "comprehensive" secondary schools, carrying larger and larger numbers from every social strata to the point of university entry, would precede the growth of mass higher education itself. In practice, however, the explosive expansion of higher education over the past two decades has almost everywhere preceded the move toward comprehensive secondary education. (The exceptions, here again, are the United States where universal comprehensive education had been achieved by World War II when enrolments in higher education were only about 15%, and Sweden where the establishment of a fully comprehensive secondary school system and the rapid move toward mass higher education have proceeded together, by plan, over the past decade.) It is more true to say that mass higher education is forcing the growth of a popular system of comprehensive secondary education rather than that the creation of the latter has made possible the expansion of higher education. (It is true, however, that the continued growth of higher education beyond, perhaps, 15% of the age grade will depend on the continued democratization of the secondary school system and the transformation of more and more terminal secondary schools into schools which qualify students for university entry.)

But the change in the principles underlying the preparation and selection of university entrants has itself proceeded through a series of phases:

i) First there was the simple principle of admitting those qualified for entry according to more or less strict meritocratic principles. This process, however, rested heavily on very marked social inequalities in the opportunities to gain those qualifications - opportunities almost exclusively offered by a small set of elite academic preparatory schools. The demand for the abolition of social inequality was in the first instance met solely by an emphasis on meritocratic procedures and criteria, without much regard for the role of social inequality in affecting the chances of meeting those criteria. Qualifications took such forms as Britian's passes in its "A" level examinations or, in other countries, the successful completion of the preparatory secondary school programme and the earning of a baccalauréat or Abitur.

ii) The set of complementary forces - increasing democratic pressures, the needs of the economy and the growth of higher education itself - lead to an expansion of those secondary schools and streams which qualify for university entry. This phase is marked by a growing concern for an increase of educational opportunities which would make it possible for "able" students from lower social strata to enter university. However, during this phase the growth in student numbers at university is very largely made up of an increase in the proportion of middle class students who almost everywhere are the first to take advantage of increases in educational opportunities of every kind and at every level.

iii) In the third phase, partly as a result of the work of sociologists and partly under political pressures, there emerges a clear and more widespread recognition of the effect of social inequalities on educational achievement. This in turn leads to special efforts to reduce the effects of such social inequalities. These take the form of proposals to modify the structure of secondary education, especially toward the comprehensive principle, or at least the extension of the educational channels through which access to higher education may be gained. In addition, there is a call for efforts to compensate for the disadvantageous effects of lower class origins. Increasingly, schools and streams that formerly led to vocational schools or simply to early termination of formal education are modified to allow, at least in principle, for the entry into university of some of their students.

iv) In the fourth stage (and in part because social inequalities show everywhere a stubbornly persistent effect on educational achievement, despite the best efforts of reformers) the egalitarians attack the selective principle of higher education and demand open access to the universities (as at Vincennes), or a greater expansion of non-university institutions of higher education which do not require the same formal academic qualifications for entry as do the universities. This phase (clearly visible in the United States though less so in European countries) marks a very significant shift from the principle of equality of opportunity for educational achievement to more radical principles of equality of educational achievement for all definable social groups and strata. The principle of equality of individual opportunity is compatible with the maintenance of meritocratic criteria for entry: the effort is to enable more students from lower social strata to meet those qualifications. The latter principle, the equality of group achievement, affirms that social justice requires that students from all social strata be equally represented among all elite groups in society, and this, at least in the short run, is incompatible with the maintenance of most meritocratic criteria for admission. Needless to say, even where put into practice, the principle of equality of group achievement is usually introduced in a highly qualified or compromised way and immediately introduces very substantial problems, among them the relation of students in open institutions to those in institutions still governed by meritocratic principles, and also the significance of the qualifications earned in institutions where meritocratic criteria have been subordinated to other values (at Vincennes, for example, the French government simply ceased to recognize its diplomas).

The question of the principles and processes of selection and admission to higher education is the crucial point at which higher education touches most closely on the social structure. What expansion does initially is to increase the opportunities for middle class children to gain an education which still promises to provide (though to a larger number of people) the dignified and rewarding professional occupations and traditional social status formerly reserved for a much smaller elite. While a detached observer might suggest that tripling or quadrupling the number of university graduates must reduce the special status and privileges accorded to the graduate, it does not so appear at the time to participants in the process - for example, the parents of the would-be university entrant. And resistance to expansion - say, from 5 to 15% of the age grade - has almost everywhere been remarkably weak in the face of democratic values and presumed economic needs. However, the "overproduction" of university graduates for the traditional graduate occupations is already causing misgivings among conservatives who see more and more clearly that mass higher education is a corrosive solvent of traditional social relations, status, hierarchies and privileged access to elite careers.

As a larger number of working class youth begins to enter university, the impact of university expansion on the life chances of upper middle class youth will become even more visible and threatening. It is hard to imagine a successful move to end the expansion of higher education, although that is certainly talked about in conservative circles in all Western countries. The establishment of different sectors of higher education reflecting the status hierarchies in the larger society is a more effective way of using higher education to buttress rather than undermine the class structure. It would be useful to examine and compare the history and development of modes of access to higher education in different advanced industrial societies in order to see how they have moved through the phases sketched here and where they are now.

It has been suggested earlier that after expansion itself, the earliest and most rapid changes in the system occur in the meaning of university student status, and in the principles of admission. Other components of the system are however more resistant and slower to change. This is because, while the decision to expand, the definition of attendance, and the rules for admission are governed largely by forces outside the university, the curriculum, the forms of administration and internal governance, the structure of the academic career, modes of instruction and academic "standards" themselves, are all largely shaped (though, again, with exceptions) more within the academy than by outside forces. These internal processes are, for better or for worse, highly conservative. This is in part because of the way universities are governed, in part because of the characteristics and orientations of academic men. Let us look briefly at the latter.

ACADEMIC ORIENTATIONS

How do academic men - the rectors and professors and associate professors, the docents and lecturers, who staff the old and the new institutions of higher education in every advanced society - view the rapid developments occurring all around them? We do not have a detailed study of the academic professions in most countries that would allow us to say with precision just how these men and women view their own institutions, students and subjects, and the great changes under way or just over the horizon. But if we cannot know the distribution of academic attitudes - the relative size and strength of the several most important positions that university teachers take toward growth and change in their institutions - we can identify the major dimensions along which those attitudes divide.

The great changes in recent decades in the size and functions of higher education have generated a diversity of orientations within the academic profession in every advanced society. Until after World War II, the small university system in most countries was staffed by professors and their assistants, men who had made or were making their careers through a life of scholarship or scientific research. The bulk of their students went into a small number of professions traditionally linked to the university degree: higher secondary school teaching, the civil service, law, medicine and the church, and in some countries into certain sectors of finance and industry. A small number of students stayed on for higher degrees as apprentices to the professors in their fields. The expansion, diversification and partial democratization of higher education over the past two decades has created different functions for higher education and in so doing has brought different kinds of students to the universities. And, as suggested earlier, within the university the old consensus about the nature and proper functions of the university has broken down; in every country academic men differ among themselves in their attitudes toward the changes in the university that are already under way or are likely to accompany further growth.

At first glance, it may seem that the major division among academic men is between those who give their approval and support to the transformation of their institutions and systems as they move from elite to mass higher education, with all the implications for selection, the curriculum, etc. , that have been discussed earlier, as opposed to those who tenaciously defend the forms and functions of elite higher education. But, in fact, many academic men (like politicians, civil servants and ordinary people) do not draw the full implications of growth nor see its logical consequences, and many support the continued expansion of higher education while opposing its transformation into mass higher education. Others are wary of growth while accepting and even supporting important changes in the character of their institutions. Thus we see that support among academics for substantial expansion, beyond 15 to 20% of the age grade in higher education, is to some degree independent of their attitudes toward the fundamental changes in governance, curriculum and the like, that we associate with the movement toward mass higher education.

In other words, an analysis of the variations in perspective and orientation among university teachers, if it is to be useful, has to combine their attitudes toward the expansion of higher education with their views about its proper character and functions. Basic differences in academic orientations are more accurately represented not along a single "traditionalist-expansionist" continuum but by a typology, one dimension of which is defined by their opposition to or support for continued rapid expansion, the other by a commitment to traditional university forms and functions versus an acceptance of the transformation of the basic functions and characteristics of the system as it moves from being an elite to being a mass system. This typology is shown graphically in the following table.

ATTITUDES REGARDING THE PROPER FORMS AND FUNCTIONS OF HIGHER EDUCATION	ATTITUDES TOWARD THE GROWTH OF HIGHER EDUCATION	
	Elitists	Expansionists
Traditionalists	I	II
Reformers	III	IV

These stark polarities do not, of course, do justice to the complex views and attitudes held by individual university teachers. Nor do they capture the nuances of thought and feeling by which men manage to maintain conceptions of the universities and of their academic roles which reflect both expansionist and elitist values, or which accept some changes but not others in the character of their institutions. Nevertheless, men do differ in the emphasis they place on these values, the priorities they put on their embodiment in university organisations, and in the allocation of both national and personal resources. It is this relative emphasis in their values and orientations that is crucial during a period of expansion and change, when men can oppose, or attempt to delay, or welcome, or even try to accelerate the changes which are associated with the expansion and democratization of higher education.

Recognizing, therefore, that any such typology is meant to be an analytical aid to understanding broad patterns of development in higher education rather than an effort to characterize individual men and their views, it may be useful to examine the types of academic orientations generated by these dimensions.

1. TRADITIONALIST-ELITIST

This complex of values and attitudes was the dominant orientation of European academic men (and, indeed, of nearly everyone who had views about universities) before World War II. In many countries they are still held by a large number of university teachers, especially the senior professors. In their purest forms they are rarely articulated or defended now in speech or print, but their power lies in the extent to which they continue to guide action. They are reflected most clearly in the work of senior academic men in their senates and committees, defending deeply held and cherished values which for some represent the very essence of the university, values which give meaning and substance to civilized society. In this view, the function of higher education is to prepare small numbers of very able and ambitious students who have been rigorously educated in highly selective elite secondary schools - lycées or gymnasiums - for the professions traditionally requiring a university degree, and to prepare an even smaller number for a life of scholarship and scientific research. This university is defined by its traditional curriculum and governed by senior professors as an autonomous corporate body. Graduates of the university, whether they remain there as scholars or go into the learned professions, should hold a distinctive status in society, and indeed comprise a special estate marked by a way of life and thought as well as by the dignities and privileges of their status. This conception of the university has its roots in the classical and humane studies of the medieval and post-medieval universities, as modified and extended by the inclusion of natural science in departments and research institutes during the 19th century. But this orientation is incompatible with the "democratic" view that entry to the university should be governed by strictly meritocratic criteria rather than by social origins and thus in principle should be open to students from every social stratum, although in practice the nature of selection and preparation for entry effectively restricts membership almost wholly to the children of the professional and upper middle classes.

In an egalitarian age, men who hold these views are often attacked as reactionary defenders of their own special privileges. But, when they defend the values of scholarship, learning and disinterested inquiry against the enormous pressures to subordinate the university to the needs of vocational training, economic growth, social levelling and contemporary politics, they are in their own minds defending an important bulwark of civilization against the new barbarism of mass society. It is an important question for societies and educators whether these views and these men will merely be defeated and "swept into the dustbin of history", or whether their views will inform and fructify the developments now occurring and survive at least in parts of the diverse systems of higher education now emerging. The fate of those values will be determined in part by the unique social and political histories of the several societies whose educational systems are now undergoing change, and in part by the ways in which these changes are accomplished. It may be that the central questions for educators in the near future will not be how to dislodge elitist-traditionalists from their positions of power in academic senates, institutes and departments, but how to preserve and defend the best of the values that they represent under conditions of mass higher education.

2. TRADITIONALIST-EXPANSIONIST

Academic men holding this position have welcomed, or at least accepted, the rapid growth of their institutions and systems while defending the traditional university values discussed above. In a word, these are men who have believed it possible to expand the elite university systems very considerably without transforming them in fundamental ways or adding to them quite different kinds of institutions - it is a belief in the expansion rather than the transformation of higher education. These views are perhaps the most widely held of the four basic orientations being described here. The pressures for expansion that followed World War II met everywhere with surprisingly little resistance from academics, in part because they recognized the changed economic and social circumstances of the post-war world; in part be cause in the short run expansion greatly increased their resources and their capacities to do many things they had wanted to do; and in part because their institutions showed a surprising capacity to carry larger numbers of students and employ more staff without a fundamental change in their character. But growth alone begins to create strains in the traditional forms and functions of higher education, and this orientation, inherently unstable, has no solution to the problems engendered by growth, except more growth or the cessation of growth.

3. ELITIST REFORMERS

This is a small but significant body of academic men who wish to preserve the unique role of universities as elite centres for scholarship and research at its highest level, but who recognize the need for certain internal reforms that would reflect the changed map of learning and the changing relationships between higher education and the larger society. Among the reforms these men have urged have been a modification of the professorial oligarchy that has governed most European universities and an improvement in the status of junior staff - in their conditions of work, their tenure and their role in departmental and university government. In addition, such men have also pressed for more support for research and a movement away from the traditional faculty toward a departmental organisation that more closely reflects the actual organisation of intellectual and scientific work; in this they have undoubtedly been influenced by the American model in which the department is the arm of the discipline in the university. In a sense, this perspective aimed to modernize the university in its organisational structure without changing its basic character as the centre for intellectual work of the highest standards, access to which is limited by meritocratic criteria to a relatively small number of able and highly motivated students. Many of these men have learned in the past few decades how much easier it is simply to increase the numbers of students and staff than to carry out the serious structural reforms that they have recommended. But, in their view, a slowing down or even a cessation in the rate of growth of higher education or the shifting of growth wholly to the non-university sectors may provide the breathing space and opportunity to reform the conditions of teaching and learning in the universities, and thus afford an opportunity for re-establishing and reinforcing those high standards threatened by the indiscriminate growth of unreformed structures.

4. EXPANSIONIST REFORMERS

Expansionist reformers, concentrated very much on the political left and among younger faculty in the social sciences and some of the arts subjects, see many of the traditional forms and functions of the university as the greatest obstacle to the democratization and expansion of higher education. The problem appears to many of them as much political as educational: to change the distribution of power within universities so as to break the capacity for resistance of the more conservative professorial elite. In this they often have the co-operation of political parties and movements, and sometimes of higher civil servants in the relevant ministries of education. The views of this body of thought are marked by a conviction that there must be a substantial transformation of higher education - that it must be extended vertically in the class structure, fundamentally democratized in its patterns of recruitment and, horizontally, it must be adapted to a broad range of social, economic and political activities of the society. For example, they want to provide useful training for a much wider range of occupations and professions than did the traditional learned professions of the old university. It is not uncommon for people with these views to link the transformation of the university to broader ideas of social transformation or revolution. Moreover, the proponents of this position do not ordinarily recommend the creation of institutions to carry these additional functions alongside the elite universities, but rather urge the transformation of those elite universities into larger, more heterogeneous, more democratic and socially responsive institutions of mass higher education. In many countries young faculty have found support for their views in the student body; the main weight of student demands for changes in the university fall into this category.

The attitudes and orientations of university teachers and administrators toward the future of higher education in their countries, summarized in this typology, both reflect and influence its growth and development. The rapid growth of higher education after World War II brought large numbers of new men into the system. In the climate of Europe at that time many of these did not accept the old assumptions of European elite education, especially its narrow class base for recruitment and the "undemocratic" rule of the professoriate.

In addition, rapid growth, both in rate and absolute numbers, weakened the close personal ties of junior and senior men which had softened and legitimated the traditional arrangements. The powerlessness and insecurity of the junior staff became more visible and more resented.

The broad-based demand for expansion set off a train of consequences most of which undermined the old assumptions and arrangements and led to calls for further democratization and reform. For example, higher education during the fifties and sixties was increasingly justified by reference to its presumed contribution to economic growth, and there was a strong emphasis on the links between university training and industrial development. At the same time, that tendency created pressures for an expansion of technological and business studies and for more directly applied research in the universities. On the other hand, the growing welfare state created a continuing demand for people with skills in the applied social sciences - in public administration, in social work, in penology - indeed for the whole range of social problems to which the state was giving increased and systematic attention. Both of these broad developments strengthened certain sections of the university and imbued them with a spirit inevitably at variance with that of the traditional elite university. Many of the problems of European higher education have centred on the accommodation of these new functions and activities - and the new kinds of people drawn to them and thus into the university - with the older functions and traditional conceptions of university life.

The typology of academic orientations sketched above, while not meant to be descriptive of the full range of views held by individual teachers and administrators, is designed to be helpful in addressing such questions as these:

- How diverse are the conceptions of academic life; are they captured in this kind of typology, or are there better ways of describing the main currents of thought among academic men about their own institutions? Do we find the same types of attitudes among politicians and civil servants, or are differences among them along different lines of cleavage?
- What is the distribution of these types within a university or a national system, and how has that distribution been changing over time?
- What is the organisational structure of this normative diversity? Do we find representatives of all of these types within every faculty, every department, in ways that are making it increasingly difficult to govern these units and carry on the ordinary business of education? Or do we find a continued consensus on the conceptions of education within faculties and departments, with the dissensus reflecting the new departments, faculties and research institutes within the expanded universities, thus leaving the two somewhat insulated from one another in the ordinary running of the institution?
- Where are the concentrations of views held in terms of subject areas, age, kind of institution and the like? New "experimental" institutions tend to recruit men interested initially in reform and expansion. Do the new institutions have much higher concentrations of "expansionist reformers", or do they increasingly become "more royalist than the king", with strongly conservative positions as a result of the insecurity of their status within their national systems of higher education?
- What are the patterns of coalition and conflict within the universities? On what kinds of issues do men and groups holding one or another of these different views join with others on such issues as curriculum reform, and to what extent are lines of conflict and cleavage drawn along these lines of academic orientations?

Briefly, we are asking whether this typology of academic orientations helps to illuminate and clarify the dynamics of conflict and change in the systems and institutions of higher education now, and whether it aids us to study and understand the evolution of these systems in the future. At the very least, if this typology shows a certain congruence with the realities of institutional life, it suggests that we need solid empirical data on the distributions of these views in different systems and parts of systems. Broad comparative survey research centring on a typology something like this may allow us to get a better sense of the role of academic attitudes and values in institutional change in European higher education. For, whatever may be the best way to discuss and analyse them, the distribution of attitudes and orientations of university teachers and administrators about their own institutions is a major force in determining whether a society moves toward mass higher education, how it deals with the strains that growth inevitably imposes before its institutions are transformed, the forms that the new mass institutions take, and whether the older functions and institutions survive and continue to perform their traditional university functions.

DILEMMAS OF GROWTH IN THE TRANSITION
TOWARD MASS HIGHER EDUCATION

The expansion of higher education and the transition from elite to mass systems generate a set of dilemmas which are not easily solved but which persist as continuing problems for teachers, students and administrators. The forms these dilemmas take and their relative importance vary from country to country, but they are visible in some form in every advanced society whose systems of higher education are growing.

Quality, Equality and Expansion

The steady expansion of higher education appears to some observers to constitute a serious threat to academic standards. The question of standards is nominally a question of the quality of an academic programme, how rigorous and demanding on the one hand, how rich and stimulating on the other. At one extreme we think of a group of learned and imaginative scholars teaching highly selected and motivated students in a situation of rich intellectual resources, cultural, scientific and academic. At the other extreme are institutions staffed by less well educated and less accomplished teachers, teaching less able and less well motivated students under less favourable conditions - marked by lower salaries, a poorer staff/student ratio, a smaller library, fewer laboratory places - and all in a less stimulating and lively intellectual environment. Many countries are committed to the expansion of their existing systems of higher education. This involves the achievement of education at a high and common standard of quality throughout the system, whatever the varied functions of the different institutions. This dual commitment - to continued growth and also to high quality in all parts of the system - poses the dilemma.

The dilemma has three components. First, there is the strong egalitarian sentiment that all provision in higher education ought to be substantially of equal quality (and thus of cost). (In the absence of good or reliable measures of the effects of higher education on the adult careers of graduates, we tend to assess the "quality" of education by reference to its internal processes, and this leads us to equate quality with cost.) The second is that the criteria against which new forms of mass higher education are assessed are typically those of the older, costlier forms of elite higher education. Third, a rapid and potentially almost unlimited growth of higher education at the per capita cost levels of the former small elite systems places intolerable burdens on national and state budgets which are also having to cope with growing demands from other public agencies, such as social welfare, pre-school education and child care, the primary and secondary school systems, housing, transportation and defence.

When applied to higher education, the egalitarian position, which cuts across class lines and party preferences, is highly critical of any tendency to institutionalize differences between the various sectors of higher education. Egalitarians in many countries are committed to closing the gulf between the several parts of their higher education systems and to reducing the differentials in the status, quality, costs and amenities of its different segments and institutions. Men with these sentiments, who might be called "unitarians" in their commitment to a single system of institutions governed throughout by common educational standards, are often also committed to reforming universities and making them serve more the functions of the non-elite forms of higher education while at the same time raising the quality of the non-elite forms, especially of higher technical education, to that of university standard. (These are the people described earlier as "expansionist reformers".) This position, liberal, humane and generous, argues that formal differentiations between the different forms and sectors of higher education almost always lead to invidious distinctions between them, and ultimately to very marked differences in the quality of their staff and students and in other respects too. Men holding these views also observe that the weaker or low status segments of the system are those characteristically associated with and used by students from working and lower middle class origins, so that the status differentiation in higher education is closely linked to that of the class structure as a whole. They argue that any sectors of education outside that system which includes the universities must necessarily be made up of second class institutions for second class (and most commonly working class) citizens, as historically has been the case. Essentially, their slogan is "nothing if not the best" - especially for youngsters from those strata of the society which have often received less or, if anything, second best.

While this position is humane and generous in its concern for equality of educational opportunities for working class people, it is, in its insistence on a "levelling upward" in cost as well as quality, inevitably in conflict with a continued and rapid expansion of the provision for higher education. No society, no matter how rich, can afford a system of higher education for 20 or 30% of the age grade at the cost levels of the elite higher education which it formerly provided for 5% of the population. Insofar as egalitarians insist that there be no major differentials in per capita costs among various sectors of the system of higher education, and at the same time insist on expansion, they force a levelling downward in costs and perhaps also in quality. Insofar as they are committed to a high and common set of standards throughout the system, they are also necessarily urging a restraint on expansion, though they themselves may not recognize this. The crucial question in this unitarian position is whether it is a commitment only to a common set of standards throughout the system, or to a common set of high standards.

The unitarian position is, I suggest, basically incompatible with very marked differences between institutions in their status, staff/student ratios and other aspects of cost and quality. While it is possible in principle to argue that some institutions would be more expensive because they carry a larger research responsibility, it is very difficult in practice to argue for a genuine unitarian system while forbidding certain parts of that system or institutions within it to engage in research. And research is inherently highly expensive. Moreover there is a tendency everywhere to identify research with the highest standards of higher education, an identification that has a strong component of reality. It is research that attracts the most able and creative academic minds, and it is the institutions that recruit these men that gain higher status in any system of higher education. Therefore a genuinely egalitarian policy must allow every institution to attract people who are innovative intellectually, and that means supporting their research and giving them the high degree of autonomy they need to create new knowledge, new fields of study and new combinations of disciplines.

These activities are very hard to rationalize and programme closely despite the new forms of systems management being introduced everywhere. For this and other reasons, a unitarian position which wishes to raise standards in all institutions to that of the leading universities tends to constrain the growth of the system: if every new place, every new institution is potentially as expensive as the most costly of the old, then growth must be very carefully planned and sharply restricted. However, where the egalitarian spirit overrides that of a commitment to high standards, as in much of the United States, the slogan is not "nothing if not the best" but rather the expansionist slogan "something is better than nothing". Under those circumstances there tends to be a levelling downward coupled with expansion rather than a levelling upward with its inherent tendencies toward a constraint on growth.

The key question in this dilemma is whether new forms of higher education can fulfil their functions at a standard that earns high status and satisfies egalitarians, while reducing per capita costs in ways that will allow genuine expansion toward mass higher education. The Open University in Great Britain is certainly one effort in that direction. Alternatively, a society may reject the arguments of the unitarians and egalitarians and develop a system on the American model that sustains internal diversity in costs and quality as well as in forms and functions. (As is suggested later, this is much more difficult in systems that are financed, and thus ultimately governed, by a central governmental agency.) In either case, the more ambitious and energetic the new institutions, the more they will demand the libraries and research facilities, the salary schedules and other amenities of the old institutions, and the more likely they are to drive their per capita costs up. It may be worth exploring how the forms of this dilemma differ in different societies.

The effect of expansion on standards and quality is a complex and uncertain issue. In the early stage of the current phase of growth, in the fifties, there was widespread concern among academics and others that the pool of talented youth able to profit from higher education was small and limited, and that expansion beyond the numbers provided by this pool would necessarily mean a decline in student quality. But this fear has declined and in some cases disappeared as numbers have grown with no demonstrable decline in overall student quality. (1) Nevertheless, some observers suggest that the new students, if not less able, are less highly motivated or less well prepared in their secondary schools for serious academic work. This feeling is widespread, though there is no good evidence to support the hypothesis and there is some reason to suspect that present-day students are being compared with idealized students in some mythical Golden Age located variously in the past, depending on the age of the speaker.

There is a somewhat more persistent and plausible concern felt by many that the rapid expansion of higher education has lowered the average quality or the adequacy of preparation of college and university teachers, especially among the new recruits. Still others fear that growth has adversely affected the relations between teachers and students, making them more remote and impersonal (where they were not so already). Others suggest that mass higher education must affect the intellectual

1. Though it appears that with larger numbers the range of student abilities is wider.

climate of colleges and universities, introducing into them the vulgarities of the market place, of vocational training, of mass politics and popular culture.

Whatever the validity of these fears, and they are not wholly without substance, it seems likely that the impact of expansion on the quality of higher education would be greatly influenced in every society by how it deals with the dilemmas discussed above, and particularly whether it strives to achieve a common level of quality throughout, or finds ways of creating and sustaining diversity within its system in all the characteristics that mark higher educational institutions, including their quality and costs. It may be that in the interaction of quality, equality and expansion, educators must accept the inequalities inherent in genuine diversity if they are to defend the highest standards of scholarly and academic life in some parts of an expanding system. But that "solution", of course, has its own costs - moral and intellectual as well as financial and political - and some societies may well opt for equality at high standards, at the cost of continued rapid expansion. It is probable, however, that only in rhetoric can all of these desirable characteristics of higher education be maximized within the same system.

PATTERNS OF PLANNING UNDER CONDITIONS
OF UNCERTAINTY AND RAPID CHANGE

An analysis of the phases of development of higher education of the kind being undertaken in this paper involves some effort to see into the future. This, of course, raises the question of the extent to which some kind of planning, either for systems or for single institutions, can help to ease the transitions and solve the problems during the transition phases uncovered by this analysis. That, in turn, involves some consideration of the nature of forecasting and the role that it may play in educational planning. Let us begin by making a distinction between secular trends and unforeseen developments.

1. SECULAR TRENDS

Secular trends, the broad movements of social institutions, the kind that we have been discussing in this paper, can reasonably be expected to continue, short of a catastrophe, over a period of decades. Among the secular trends in higher education that we can reasonably expect to continue for the rest of the century the most important are growth, democratization and diversification.

a) Growth

Despite the problems that the growth of higher education brings in its train and despite the arguments one hears from various quarters that the growth should be slowed or stopped, it seems very unlikely that any advanced industrial society can or will be able at any time in the near future to stabilize the numbers going on to some form of higher education. This is true for a number of reasons that will probably be compelling for any government or ministry.

There is almost certainly going to be a continued popular demand for an increase in the number of places in colleges and universities. Despite much loose talk about graduate unemployment or over-supply of educated men, it is still clear that people who go on to higher education thereby greatly increase their chances of having more secure, more interesting and better paid work throughout their lives. The concern of young men and women and of their parents for access to the best and most highly rewarding jobs in the society (rewarding in every sense) will insure that the demand for places continues to be high.

These rational calculations and anticipations initially affect those people (and their children) who are, so to speak, at the margin of higher education, who would a few years earlier have ended their formal education on the completion of secondary schooling. But growth and the movement from elite to mass higher education itself creates a set of social and psychological forces which tend to sustain it. As more and more people go to college or university, and as an even larger number become aware of it as a possible and reasonable aspiration for themselves and their children, higher education enters into the standard of living of growing sectors of the population. Sending one's sons and daughters to college or university increasingly becomes one of the decencies of life rather than an extraordinary privilege reserved for people of high status or extraordinary ability. Giving one's children a higher education begins to resemble the acquisition of an automobile or washing machine, one of the symbols of increasing affluence - and there can be little doubt that the populations of advanced industrial societies have the settled expectation of a rising standard of living. But, in addition, sending one's children to college or university is already, and will be more so in the future, a symbol of rising social status. Not only does it give evidence of status mobility in the adult generation - in this respect resembling the purchase of a home in the country or an automobile - but it also lays the necessary foundation for the social mobility of a family across generations. Everywhere the numbers of people who have completed secondary education grow, and as more people complete secondary education the more necessary it is for their children to go on to higher education if they are to qualify for still higher status occupations. This is increasingly the case as more and more occupations require a degree or other higher education qualification for entry.

The wishes of parents and youngsters to go on to higher education would of course be inhibited if there were no growth in the jobs that "require" post-secondary education. On this score there is presently much talk of an over-supply of graduates and of a decline in the market for people who have had further education. But there is little evidence of that over-supply, and this will certainly remain the case for the next three or four decades. For closely related to the growth of demand for places, which might be called the push from the general population, there is the pull of the economy, marked particularly by the continued growth of the tertiary or service sector of the society. This takes two forms. One is the growth of those occupations which traditionally or presently require higher educational qualifications. The growth of every advanced economy is marked by a much more rapid growth in the numbers of managerial and technical personnel than of manual or skilled workers. The rationalization of production and the growth of industrial and commercial organisations generate enormous bureaucratic structures which in their middle and higher reaches clearly call for the skills, attitudes and orientations that are provided by post-secondary education. Moreover, there is a whole range of new and semi-professions, particularly those linked to the welfare functions of government - the social workers, penologists, experts in environment, transport, housing and urban problems - which call for advanced training.

In addition, and equally important, is the educational inflation of occupations. As the supply of educated people grows, job requirements are redefined so that occupations which formerly were filled by secondary school graduates are increasingly restricted to people with post-secondary education. It may be argued that many of these jobs - for example, the middle levels of business management or public administration - do not need formal post-secondary education. But, in fact, growing numbers of people with more formal education compete successfully for these jobs with people who have less formal qualifications. Once in those jobs, they tend to reshape them by exercising responsibility, taking initiative and applying skill and imagination in ways that the job may not have "required" when it was being filled by people with lower qualifications. This is an aspect of the impact of the extension of higher education on the occupational structure that manpower analysts almost never take into account, partly because until recently graduates had been going into traditional graduate occupations rather than redefining and reshaping jobs formerly filled by people who had not been to college or university. One of the most important aspects of the movement from elite to mass higher education lies precisely in this transformation of jobs by people of greater education than were employed formerly in those jobs.

What mass higher education does is to break the old rigid connection between education and the occupational structure under which a degree not only qualified men for a certain range of occupations and professions but also disqualified them for all the jobs which formerly did not employ graduates. Thus "graduate unemployment" has never meant that graduates could not get jobs in competition with non-graduates, but that they could not get the kind of jobs that they thought appropriate to their status and dignity. The growth of mass higher education breaks this connection and allows people who have gained a higher education to seek employment, without loss of dignity, wherever the jobs may exist. By entering the job market without prior conceptions of "inappropriate" jobs, graduates can up-grade the jobs that they do take, both in status and in the scope they give for the application of skill and initiative. At the same time, by competing with those who have not been through college or university they increase the pressures on the latter to gain formal qualifications so that they too can compete successfully for the same range of white collar occupations. This process (like the rising standard of living as applied to formal education) is one of the processes which inexorably increases the demand for higher education both from the populations of industrial societies and from their occupational structures.

Alongside these social, psychological and economic forces are the institutional changes in secondary education which bring more and more students to the point of college or university entry. The raising of the school-leaving age, the broad extension of university preparatory studies, the spread of comprehensive schooling, are all institutional encouragements to students to stay on longer and to qualify for entry to college or university. The extension of educational opportunities in secondary education reflects both the fundamental democratization of modern society and changes in the economy mentioned earlier. But it works independently of these other forces to increase the pool of young men and women "at the margin" of higher education - and thus the absolute numbers and the proportion of the age grade - who are able to pursue further studies in response to a variety of other economic and social motivations.

It is widely recognized that the rate of social, economic and technological change in modern societies is very high and is increasing. Inventions such as the computer, changes in the supply of energy implicit in nuclear fission and fusion, changes in forms of transportation and entertainment and communication, all create new industries almost overnight while sentencing others to rapid decay and obsolescence. The more highly developed the economy, the more rapid these transformations of the economy and its underlying technological base, and all of this in turn forces changes throughout life on people in the labour force. One student of social and technological change has estimated that a man who is presently entering the labour market in the United States will change not just his job but the industry in which he works nine or ten times in the course of his working life.

The rapidity of social change, largely though not exclusively due to rapid technological change, puts a very great premium on the ability to learn over the mastery of specific skills. This, in turn, greatly increases the functional importance of formal schooling over apprenticeship or on-the-job training. Formal education provides a base of broad understanding of managerial and technical principles and, above all, a training in the capacity to acquire new knowledge; while apprenticeship and on-the-job training more often transmit skills which are likely very quickly to become obsolescent. Rapid technological and organisational change loosen the links between formal education and specific parts of the occupational structure; but they increase the role of formal schooling in underpinning the whole structure of a rapidly changing technological system. This fact argues against the widespread assumption that "non-technical" studies have no vocational component. On the contrary, it is likely that the most important "skill" acquired in higher education is the capacity to respond sensitively and successfully to rapid social and technological change. Above any specific skill acquired, it is this that students in colleges and universities gain in their higher studies which gives them a significant advantage over those who have not been through higher education. Indeed, it may well be that formal education is the major determinant of whether men and women are the beneficiaries or the victims of social and economic changes.

It is clear that these changes benefit some sections of the population while hurting others, and those hurt most are those with inflexible skills who have not the capacity to adapt readily to new requirements or opportunities. It is not only the ability to adapt to new jobs but the capacity to learn where new opportunities are arising that is the mark of the educated man, and this is a very great advantage that he has over less well-educated people in contemporary societies.

b) Democratization

One secular trend in modern times - a movement that in Western countries is unbroken for at least two centuries and shows no signs of weakening - is the fundamental democratization of society. In its earliest forms this involved the extension of the franchise and other aspects of political power to larger and larger sections of the society. In addition, there has been a continued weakening of traditional social distinctions and the extension of various social and economic rights (which were once privileges) to ever broader sections of the community. Traditional social hierarchies still survive and patterns of deference are deeply imbedded in the social structures of many societies. Nevertheless, everywhere in the West they are weakening under the impact of world wars, the growth of the consuming society, and the levelling forces of democratic politics, the mass media and mass education. The movement toward mass higher education will contribute to this fundamental democratization of society, but also the democratization of society will feed back upon and contribute to the extension of educational opportunities. But the expansion and democratization of educational opportunity, the opening of doors, so to speak, is only part of this process. Sooner or later the argument is made that the ultimate results of a policy of equality of opportunity must be visible in the equality of achievement of social groups and strata.

If intelligence is randomly distributed in a population - an empirical question which has come to be a political affirmation - then any differences in the proportions of youth from different social groups or strata who enter higher education and gain its degrees and certificates must be due to patterns of social discrimination and not to variations in individual ability. These differences in an egalitarian age are increasingly defined as inequities and the product of injustice, and very strong social and political forces are at work to reduce or obliterate them. The net result of these forces must be the expansion of places, if the proportions from every social class are to be equalized. This is clearly more a long-range goal than any immediately achievable outcome of public policy; moreover, there are many arguments of principle against these policies. Whatever one may think of those arguments, however, it is difficult to imagine that they will be decisive and that the fundamental democratization of the society will not also extend to the provision of places in higher education, as it has for primary schooling and is in the process of doing at the secondary levels.

c) <u>Diversification</u>

Another broad trend in higher education that we might reasonably expect to continue is the diversification of the forms and functions of higher education. As already suggested several times in this paper, the growth of numbers has also meant an increasing diversity of students with respect to their social origins and other characteristics, their motivations, aspirations, interests and adult careers. All of this places great pressures on the system to reflect the diversity of students in a similar diversity of educational provision - in the curriculum, in forms of instruction and the like. A central issue is the continuing struggle on the part of more traditionally oriented educators against the threat, as they see it, to standards, values, and indeed the very essence of the traditional university, posed by the pressures for diversification arising out of the growing and changing student population.

In addition to the familiar changes within the "regular" colleges and universities, there is also a movement to diversify higher education upward and outward: upward to provide adult education or lifelong learning for a very large part of the adult population; outward, to bring it to people in their own homes or workplaces. The pressures behind this are many. There is obviously the force of rapid social and technological change which alone creates a need for the provision of new skills or renewed formal training for people who are changing their occupations, or whose jobs and professions are changing more rapidly than their capacity to keep up through on-the-job experience. For example, engineers and doctors become increasingly out of touch with the latest developments in their professions unless they are able to get formal refresher training during their professional careers. But, in addition, many educators are noting that substantial sections of the old university student body entering directly from secondary school are for various reasons somewhat resentful of their prolonged formal education and rather weakly motivated. By contrast, the motication of adults already in the occupational structure for further formal education is often very high. They are much more rewarding to teach and indeed bring a new and stimulating element back into the classroom by way of their own job experience. In addition they tend to be less highly politicized and have a more exclusively academic or vocational interest, and this appeals to many educators as well as to politicians. Add to this the fact that adult education, offered part-time or in the evenings for people already in the occupational structure, often turns out to be less expensive than traditional forms of higher education. The students do not have to be expensively maintained in halls of residence; moreover, there is not the hidden cost of their foregone earnings if they are actually at work while attending college or university courses. A great deal has been written on the subject of permanent education; I share the view of many that this may well be the sector of higher education which grows the most rapidly over the next three or four decades. If adults are brought directly into the central college and university facilities and are taught alongside young men and women directly out of secondary school, it may be enormously beneficial for both sides and in important respects change the character of higher education for the older and younger groups alike.

Adult education, already liberated from the traditional forms associated with the education of young men and women, is likely to break with all sorts of traditional assumptions about how higher education is accomplished. It is likely to be more dispersed and brought much closer to where people live and work. Already the Open University in Britain has demonstrated that higher education at the high standard of British universities can be offered to men and women in their own homes, and this is a lesson that is being learned by similar forms of off-campus and "extended" education in the United States and other countries. The imaginative use of television, of video cassettes and remote computer consoles will greatly facilitate the provision of higher education outside the traditional boundaries of the university or college buildings. And while these developments are likely to occur first in connection with adult education, they may very well be adapted to the education of post-secondary youth in the near future.

Growth, democratization, diversification, these are the secular trends in higher education that we can anticipate continuing over the next three or four decades, though at different rates and in different forms in different places. If the future were the product of the secular trends alone we could plan for it with some assurance, some sense of our capacity to master the future, first intellectually and then institutionally. But the future is not just the aggregate of secular trends; it is also full of unforeseen events and developments which sharply limit our power to anticipate the nature of the world for which we plan, or our capacity to make our plans achieve the results that we intend.

2. UNFORESEEN DEVELOPMENTS

Unforeseen developments take a number of different forms, such as new techniques and technologies in industries, specific and enormously consequential historical events, and broad changes in the values of sections of the society and most especially of youth. Who could have forecast only two or three decades ago the development of the computer industry or of electronics more generally? These industries have affected the economies and occupational structures of advanced industrial societies very considerably, and in a narrower perspective they have greatly changed the resources available to education. Video cassettes, television, computers and the like make it possible at least to imagine extended forms of higher education very different from the correspondence courses of the "external degree" before World War II.

Specific historical events also affect our power to forecast the development of institutions. In America the assassinations of John and Robert Kennedy changed the politics (and the colleges and universities) of that nation profoundly, not least through their effect on the extent and duration of America's military involvement in Indo-China. The balance of payments crisis in Britain and its effect on the British National Plan in the late sixties very substantially modified the development of higher education in that country. Or, to take a more speculative example, a substantial easing of tensions between East and West and a very sharp control of the arms race may in the future release for higher education substantial resources in Western countries which are now spent on defence.

There are also broad changes in values, in whole societies or in major segments, which affect higher education. For example, the quite unanticipated growth of concern for the environment in all industrial societies will affect higher education in various ways - on the one hand increasing the demand for people with broad combinations of advanced learning in social and technical areas, on the other hand providing important additional competition for resources that might otherwise go to higher education. Another example is the growth of the "counter culture" in every Western society, and what is clearly a retreat from reason among sections of middle class youth toward neoromanticism and unconventional forms of religiosity. Closely related to this there is among certain sections of youth what might be called a crisis of ambition, marked by the primacy of moral considerations and a "quest for community" as against the striving for individual achievement and a personal career. These changes in values, the significance of which is hard to assess over the long run, may have very great consequences for institutions such as universities that are founded so substantially on the rule of reason and on the preparation for adult careers based on knowledge and expertise.

The heightened political concerns of university students in the late sixties, and the readiness to carry political activism into the university itself, have posed another set of problems for institutions of higher education, and it is difficult to know how that pattern will develop in the decades ahead. In addition there are changes in the relations between the generations, in the strength and basis of authority and in a whole variety of fundamental beliefs and values which make problematic the traditional forms of relationships in colleges and universities.

3.   FORMS OF "PLANNING"

In the face of so much that is so problematic and fortuitous in historical development, as against what can reasonably be anticipated as the outcome of foreseeable secular change, it is useful to make a distinction between what might be called "prescriptive planning" and "systems planning".

Prescriptive planning, the kind that is most commonly practised by the governing agencies and ministries of advanced societies, aims to spell out in detail the size and shape of the higher education system over the next several decades, and the content and forms of instruction - in brief, what will be taught, to whom, to how many, in what kind of institutions and at what expense. Prescriptive planning necessarily rests on an analysis of secular trends (and only some of those). Typically, it bases itself on estimates and projections of the demand for higher education, both in the population at large and by the economy, and the resources available to higher education over a period of years. Systems planning, by contrast, would have as its aim the evolution of a system of higher education marked by diversity and flexibility. It would not aim to specify in detail what those institutions of higher education would look like, or how and what they would teach to whom. The difference in these modes of planning is between planning the specific size, shape and content of an educational system, and planning the structure or form of a system of higher education which is best able to respond to the combination of secular trends and unforeseen developments.

The forces for prescriptive planning are dominant everywhere, despite the fact that they are probably inappropriate for a future that inevitably involves unforeseen developments. They are dominant first because of the very existence of agencies of central control. The existence of a central state administrative apparatus with the power to plan prescriptively is the first guarantee that that will be the form planning will take. There is, in addition, the illusion that higher education constitutes a closed system relatively impervious to unforeseen developments. This is a hangover from the period when almost the whole of education consisted of compulsory schooling plus a very small system of elite higher education; the bulk of planning for that kind of system was largely a planning for space and for the number of teachers necessary for a known population of youngsters. The forms and patterns of broad, nationwide prescriptive planning for primary and secondary education are now being adapted to higher education. Yet it is easy to see how much more vulnerable higher education is to unforeseen developments in technology, historical events and broad changes in values than is the system of primary and secondary education. Third, growth itself stimulates prescriptive planning: the more higher education grows, the more money is needed for it, the more interest there is in it among larger parts of the population, the greater demand there is for tight control over its shape and costs. The growing demand for accountability of higher education, for its ability to demonstrate its efficiency in the achievement of mandated and budgeted goals, inevitably translates itself into tighter controls and prescriptive planning. But this control can only be exercised rationally in terms of available knowledge based on foreseeable trends and projections. The growth of higher education, given a prescriptive control system, places ever greater demands on that system to maintain and increase its control over numbers and costs, structures and standards.

Prescriptive planning involving that kind of close control has however very little flexibility to respond to the unforeseen, and a very slow response rate to new developments. In addition, it politicizes many educational issues by locating the key decisions in central political agencies. But, perhaps most important, prescriptive planning by central planning agencies does not and perhaps cannot create genuine diversity in the forms and structures of higher education, although diversity itself constitutes the major resource that higher education has for responding to the unforeseen as well as to the anticipated developments and secular trends of modern society.

Central governing bodies tend to exert pressures toward uniformity among the institutions under their control. These tendencies are only slowed by the formal allocation of different functions to different sectors and are not reversed, as they are for example in Britain's "binary" system. There are several pressures for uniformity or convergence associated with central governmental control over higher education:

   i) the uniform application of administrative forms and principles, as in formulas linking support to enrolments, formulas governing building standards and the provision and allocation of space, formulas governing research support, etc.;
   ii) broad norms of equity, which prescribe equal treatment for "equivalent" units under a single governing body;
   iii) increasingly strong egalitarian values which define all differences among public institutions - in their functions, standards and support - as inequitable.

96

Add to these the tendency for institutions to converge toward the forms and practices of the most prestigious models of higher education, a tendency which operates independently of government control, and we see that the forces working against diversity in higher education are very strong at a time when expansion increases the needs for diversification of forms and functions beyond that which presently exists.

In many countries the struggle to contain diversity takes the form of an effort to maintain tight controls over standards, costs, functions, forms and so forth, all in the service of the traditional values of higher education. Diversity is seen not only as a threat to the power of the state over a major claimant on public resources, as a threat to orderly governmental and bureaucratic process and as a challenge to the norms of equity and equality; diversity is also seen as academic anarchy and a threat to the traditional values of higher education itself.

There is here in part a hostility to the market which is seen, correctly, as subversive of prescriptive controls and as embodying the mastery of the unqualified over what ought to be a protected sphere of cultural life. Add to this the relation of growth to high costs and public accountability, and the consequent rationalization of administration in the service of efficiency, and we see how strong are the forces making for prescriptive planning. Everywhere one sees the distaste of central governmental agencies for the messiness and unpredictability of genuine and evolving diversity, and their continued efforts to bring their systems back under control and along desired lines of development. One may ask whether that tendency, which emerges more strongly during the confusions and uncertainties of transition from elite to mass higher education, is in fact likely to produce the kind of diverse system appropriate to mass higher education.

There are counter forces which help to sustain and even increase diversity in higher education (and these, of course, vary in strength in different countries). In some places there is a multiplicity of governmental bodies involved in higher education: the United States is an extreme case in this respect. More generally, there are variations in the degree of diversity of sources of support, both of public and private funds. Third, the desirability of diversity of forms and functions in higher education is being increasingly recognized by politicians and educators, and this leads to efforts to create and defend these institutional differences through legislative and budgetary means. (1) In addition, there is a growing sense of the inadequacy of the existing educational forms and a growing readiness to provide support for educational innovations on every level of higher education. Perhaps most important, rapid growth and large size make it more difficult for governing agencies to impose uniform patterns in systems already very large and diverse.

The growth of institutions and systems toward mass higher education puts a strain on administrative structures designed for a smaller, simpler, elite system, and activities begin to elude the controls of an overburdened and understaffed administration. Finally, whether or not it is desirable, it is difficult to rationalize the multiplicity of functions and activities that go on within higher education. Much of what is done

1. This effort to achieve diversity through prescriptive planning runs against the political forces of equality, the bureaucratic preferences for standardization, and the academic tendency of institutions to model themselves on the most prestigious. This is an intent of the "binary" policy in Britain. For a discussion of its recent problems see the comments of its author, Anthony Crosland, in the Times Higher Education Supplement, 6th June 1972.

in higher education is esoteric and hard to understand for anyone outside a narrow academic or professional speciality. This near monopoly
within the academic world of specialized knowledge about the nature of
the academic fields, their needs and requirements, is the ultimate basis
of academic autonomy and slows (though it may not prevent) rationalization and the application of standardized formulas governing admissions,
academic standards, support, workloads, etc. (This is, of course, the
more true where the knowledge base is greater and the intellectual authority of the academics concerned is higher - which is why academic
autonomy is defended more successfully in elite institutions.)

The multiplicity of academic activities and the specialized knowledge required to assess or evaluate them interferes also with the flow
to the top management of an institution of accurate and standardized
information about what is going on within it, and this is particularly true
for higher governmental agencies and authorities. The resulting areas
of ignorance and obscurity make it more difficult to develop standardized
procedures and formulas, and thus sustain diversities.

Systems planning, by contrast, would aim to strengthen the forces
making for diversity in higher education. It would, for example, increase the range and diversity of governing agencies and sources of support; it would encourage an increase in the range of functions performed
and constituencies served by the system (though not necessarily by an
individual institution); it would create forms of budgetary control in the
service of accountability that do not impose the same formulas, standards,
or criteria of "efficient performance" on all parts of the system. It
would, in the terms of this paper, defend elite institutions in an emerging
system of mass higher education without allowing the old elite institutions
to impose their forms, standards and costs on the new institutions or on
the system as a whole.

Planning for a system marked by diversity runs against the habits
and structures of educational planning in most European countries. Planning for diversity clearly involves risks, whereas prescriptive planning
gives the illusion of meeting a contingent future more effectively (though
quite possibly the reverse is true). Prescriptive planning and the central
administrative and control structures which make it possible are, as
suggested earlier, the enemies of diversity because diversity makes
prescriptive planning and control more difficult and because it violates
the principles of equitable treatment by government agencies and equality
of status of public institutions. For these and other reasons it seems
unlikely that those governmental agencies which have the responsibility
for higher education can or will surrender their control.

Thus, on balance, it would appear that in most European countries
the forces working against genuine diversity in higher education are
rather stronger than those working to sustain or increase it. This may
be debatable, in which case it is an issue which deserves further comparative study. But if that assumption is true, then several questions deserve close attention:

    i) Is increasing control over the forms and functions of higher
       education by central public agencies or authorities an inevit-
       able concomitant of expansion and increased costs?

   ii) Is the (increasing) role of public authorities presently a force
       working against diversity in higher education, in their functions
       and standards, their modes of governance, their forms of
       instruction, their sources of support and their relation to other
       institutions of society?

  iii) If so, are these "standardizing" tendencies inherent in central
       governmental control, or is it possible for central governing

and financing agencies to function in ways that sustain and increase the diversity in higher education? If so, what governing and funding structures would have that effect, and what principles of operation would govern their activities? How can efforts to support diversity be sustained against the political pressures in almost all advanced industrial societies arising out of (a) the norms which prescribe equitable treatment of all comparable units and (b) growing egalitarian sentiments and policies?

CONCLUSION

Needless to say, it is impossible to say anything very specific that would be at the same time true for all the emerging forms of higher education in 15 or 20 complex industrial societies. Therefore, to say anything that might be useful, or at least interesting, it is necessary to carry the discussion onto a somewhat higher level of abstraction. But this means, as suggested earlier, that the remarks made cannot be true in detail for any institution or even any single national system.

Moreover, this paper is not intended to increase or disseminate knowledge in the way, for example, that a statistical report or comparative survey of some emerging educational patterns does. It is rather an effort to suggest a way of thinking about the development of higher education in advanced societies, and to provide a way of framing a set of interrelated questions about this development. Many of my apparently confident assertions will be challenged, and some may in fact be empirically wrong, at least in places. But that is less important than whether the questions thus raised, the problems and issues thus identified, are in fact the problems, issues, dilemmas of higher education that educators and politicians, students and citizens, face in societies whose systems of higher education are moving from elite to mass forms. The aim of the paper was to help identify and clarify those questions, and not to answer them. In keeping with my evident bias in favour of diversity, I can only hope that even if the questions that higher education in advanced societies face are similar, their answers will be different.

Part Two

GUIDELINES FOR DISCUSSION

by
the OECD Secretariat

I

ACCESSIBILITY TO POST-SECONDARY EDUCATION AND EMPLOYMENT

INTRODUCTION

The future development of post-secondary education is faced with a number of uncertainties, particularly in relation to the size and nature of the demand, the amount of available resources and the possibilities for graduates to find suitable employment. These uncertainties may to a large extent be ascribed to the difficulties involved in devising and introducing structural reforms.

One of the crucial problems facing the authorities whose task it is to promote structural reforms in post-secondary education, in the absence of any prescriptive planning measures which would give the system a precise orientation, is to reconcile individual demand with the requirements in skills and qualifications. It is no easy task to reconcile such inherently different objectives. Nevertheless this could perhaps be achieved by introducing new admission policies and procedures, by modifying the structure and organisation of studies and by incorporating into education a more clearly defined vocational component.

The purpose of this paper is to give a brief outline of the major trends in the development of higher education from the point of view of the problems of access and of the relationship between higher education and employment. Finally, a number of questions will be put forward for discussion.

DEVELOPMENT OF HIGHER EDUCATION AND PROBLEMS OF ACCESSIBILITY

The development of higher education in OECD Member countries has been governed by various objectives. In most cases, the primary objective has been to cope with individual demand while at the same time endeavouring to achieve other aims, particularly that of promoting equality of educational opportunity. The first of these objectives would appear to have been achieved and the demand satisfied thanks to a rapid increase in the resources allocated to this sector and to a considerable expansion of intake capacities. However, the size and nature of this demand, particularly in Europe, remain to a large extent determined by the selection processes operating during secondary education. A number of higher educational establishments stipulate additional entry requirements which tend to reinforce certain disparities in participation; but these mainly influence the distribution of graduates of long-cycle secondary education among various branches or types of study and do not prevent the vast majority of them from embarking on higher educational courses.

During the past fifteen years, many reforms of secondary education have been introduced in Europe. At lower secondary level, certain structural rigidities have been eliminated and unduly early streaming has been postponed. Though these changes have helped to increase and to diversify the potential demand for higher education, they have affected neither the structure of upper secondary education (except in the case of Sweden) nor the procedures and principles governing admission to higher education. There is still a sharp division in upper secondary education between general or technical streams leading to higher studies, and vocationally oriented streams which in general preclude the continuation of further studies. The choice of secondary level courses constitutes a form of preliminary streaming into certain types or branches of higher education. Moreover, the prestige attached to certain long-cycle university courses and the professions to which they lead helps to maintain a strong demand for the general secondary streams which prepare students for these courses. This state of affairs helps to accentuate the radical distinctions between the various upper secondary streams and to reinforce certain inequalities related to social background or to sex which influence the student's choice of course.

Measures to rectify this situation - for example offering graduates of vocational secondary education, or even people who have not completed their secondary schooling, the possibility of going on to higher education - have had little effect. The expansion of higher education has resulted from the growth in the number of graduates of long-cycle secondary courses who, not having received any training which leads directly to a job, frequently have no choice but to embark upon higher studies.

This expansion has most frequently occurred within the traditional structures of the system. It has not radically affected the traditional admission criteria, particularly in the case of European universities, nor the structure of those studies designed to prepare the elite of secondary level students for a small number of professions enjoying high social status. Certainly the pattern of student choice has altered slightly, but attempts to adapt this, even in the aggregate, to the qualification requirements and to the available employment opportunities have by and large failed. Students have preferred to embark upon long-cycle post-secondary courses despite the efforts made to develop short-cycle studies, many turning away from scientific and technical disciplines in favour of the humanities.

At the same time, expansion has generated situations which call for completely new political initiatives. Higher education is today intended for a new and much more heterogeneous student "clientele" composed of young people and adults whose backgrounds, interests and individual aptitudes widely differ.

The development of mass education calls for radical reforms and in particular for great diversification of curricula designed to meet the greater range of needs and interests. In most systems, however, and especially in Europe, the major remaining political problem is the adjustment of conditions of access to post-secondary education. This is in fact the problem of selection. It is difficult to deny that some form of selection is unavoidable; the crucial problem is to replace the present, irreversible selection process which is based on social criteria and which continues to operate throughout secondary education, by a new, more equitable method offering the various social groups (young people and particularly adults) more equal opportunities of access to higher education; a method which is more acceptable to society as a whole and one which can be applied throughout the lifetime of the individual.

Ultimately, the solutions which are adopted to attain such an aim are linked to political priorities reflecting the hierarchy of goals assigned to the education system and the preferences of society or the state in the matter of education. More specifically, the reform of selection procedures will result in changes in the nature of qualifications (scholastic and other) required for access to higher education, in available intake capacities (with special reference to the application of numerus clausus) and in methods of selection, either inside the higher education establishments (examinations, tests, orientation and self-assessment of results, quotas, lotteries) or outside them (during secondary education or in the course of professional employment).

POST-SECONDARY EDUCATION
IN RELATION TO EMPLOYMENT

The primary feature of the transformation of the employment pattern is a growing demand for skills. This explains the difficulties experienced today by young graduates, particularly those who have received a general university education, in finding employment commensurate with their qualifications. Since the number of high-level posts has not increased at the rate at which higher education has developed, there is currently a fear of under-employment or depreciation of degrees ("downward mobility"). But, will the flow of graduates in its turn not give rise to new development trends in the pattern of employment? The availability of better educated, more highly skilled personnel gives promise of a new increase in productivity and this "inflow of brains" might be expected to boost the dynamism of the economic structures, thereby leading to a fuller satisfaction of social needs.

The development of education has, in fact, resulted in a change of the renewal mechanisms in all occupational sectors. Longer schooling contributes to turning the younger generation away from industrial employment and in particular from manual work. The development of education has helped to foster the theoretically oriented occupational sectors and functions to the detriment of others which sometimes call for skills that are more complex and more difficult to acquire. Looking beyond mere statistics, one might question the extent to which the development of education has helped to raise the average level of skills. (1)

For some years a new phenomenon has been emerging, that is the fact that a degree or diploma is no longer a guarantee of employment. Young graduates are affected by unemployment. Should one conclude that there are too many graduates, more in fact than can be absorbed by the economy? Should present-day difficulties be attributed to excessive vocational ambitions on their part? Or are such employment difficulties to be seen as a sign that formal education is not geared to the needs of employment?

In several countries (Sweden, United States, United Kingdom) some of these difficulties could rightly be ascribed to an unfavourable economic

---

1. The term "skill" is taken in the general sense of an aptitude to contribute effectively to the satisfaction of society's real needs.

situation. It is also possible that the rapid increase in the supply of graduates has made their integration into the labour force difficult, the economic structures being unable to absorb them straightaway. Moreover, some of these diplomas are awarded for new courses or by new institutions which are unfamiliar to employers or which provide training in skills for which the demand is still limited. Lastly, it may well be that salaries offered to young graduates have been judged to be inadequate and discouraged them from taking a job immediately. The extensive possibilities of substitution of different graduates for a single job, which has been recorded by several surveys, suggests that in the long term the economy possesses a fairly extensive absorption capacity in this respect. It thus seems premature to speak of an over-production of graduates, and it is debatable whether this argument could be put forward to justify measures designed to limit access to higher education. Over and beyond this, however, the difficulties facing graduates would appear to call in question certain structural imbalances which might be attributed (i) to a failure to gear the vocational component of higher training courses to corresponding occupations, and (ii) to the lack of co-ordination of admission policies among the various branches of higher education and also the lack of harmonization between the content of these various training courses and the corresponding admission policies.

The trend towards vocationally oriented mass higher education obliges governments to face the concrete problem of <u>defining and introducing a vocational component into education,</u> (1) at both the upper secondary level and the higher level where in most countries vocational education and general education are too rigidly differentiated. It appears necessary today to make the content of education more directly relevant to working life; emphasis is everywhere laid on the need for more practical <u>training</u> and for better planned <u>specialization</u>, less exclusively focused upon research. The concern to make education vocationally oriented raises the further question of defining "clusters of skills" as a basis for admission policies. Until now, <u>numerus clausus</u> has frequently been the only procedure proposed in this connection.

Lastly, one of the causes of the present imbalance between education and employment undoubtedly lies in the autonomous development of the educational system and in the absence of any appropriate mechanisms to co-ordinate education and employment. The incorporation of a vocational component into higher education presupposes the development of closer links between education and employment, either at the policy-making level or at the institutional level. This trend can be observed in short-cycle or part-time post-secondary courses but seldom relates to the higher education system as a whole.

THEMES FOR DISCUSSION

The attempt to reconcile various objectives:

- by adapting admission policies and procedures,
- by modifying the structure and organisation of studies,

1. This vocational component in education should be balanced by the introduction of an educational component into work; this educational component would be reflected in the conception of employment and career as well as in further training policies.

- by incorporating a more clearly defined vocational component into education,

leads to the following themes for discussion:

i) In most European Member countries one of the major problems is to co-ordinate admission procedures among the various branches of higher education and to better adapt them to the new student clientele. The need for student <u>selection</u> is an inevitable one, justified both by the existence of financial constraints and by the concern to bring the development of higher education under control and to meet more fully the needs of specific groups (adults, for example).

ii) The various proposed changes in admission policies should be considered: for example, the strengthening or adjustment of current regulations, the establishment of different orientation cycles, self-assessment for students, the introduction or extension of <u>numerus clausus</u>, and the application of new procedures (quotas, lotteries and so forth). The harmonization of these various methods throughout the educational system (for example, between long university education and short-cycle studies) has become a matter of vital importance.

iii) The effects of each of these selection methods must be evaluated. If the aim is to promote procedures that are both equitable and effective, the criterion of <u>efficacy</u> will probably tend to select the best qualified and most highly motivated candidates whose chances of successfully completing the course are greatest; while the concern for <u>equity</u> will tend to foster the admission of students from all groups and particularly from those which up till now have frequently been eliminated by existing selection methods (adults, women, young people from underprivileged social groups or minorities).

iv) The concept of qualification for admission to post-secondary education should be redefined. At present it is based on academic criteria: the acquisition of general knowledge and the award of a secondary school-leaving certificate. The introduction of reforms in upper secondary education together with the proposed incorporation of a vocational component, i. e. courses designed to prepare students for higher education, should help to modify this concept of qualification. Its content should also be broadened to take into account the acquisition of occupational skills (for the admission of adults) and of other than purely academic criteria.

v) An essential feature of the new admission policies is the diversification of options, channels of access and the structure of studies. Several measures have been introduced for this purpose: the reform of the first years of study (e. g. the Diplôme d'études universitaires générales in France (DEUG)), the restructuring of curricula in terms of units (credits), the extension of the range of options and opportunities to return to the education system, increased possibilities of transfer between the different types of course, and the creation of new education institutions are but a few examples. This diversification should make it possible to satisfy all types of demands and in particular those from adults.

vi) The restructuring of studies, which is a vital issue, raises the problem of the distribution of students within the system and the extent to which it corresponds to the employment structure. The solution to this problem lies partly in developing orientation and guidance policies and in extending student information services on courses and the openings to which they lead.

vii) The introduction of a vocational component into all higher education courses has become an essential issue in mass education. It involves rethinking such traditional principles as the division of courses according to discipline, the progressive organisation of studies, the primacy of theory over practice and the definition and use of specialization as a pedagogical tool. If education is to meet currently conflicting demands, a whole new conception will have to be evolved and implemented.

viii) Lastly, consideration will have to be given to the arrangements necessary to ensure that employment conditions and requirements are taken into account - at the policy-making stage or at the institutional level - in relation to local conditions. Although such mechanisms already exist in the Member countries, they are often insufficiently developed to permit any interpretation of the specified skill requirements or to provide an overall picture of society's needs and the dynamics of employment.

II

NON-TRADITIONAL FORMS OF STUDY
IN POST-SECONDARY EDUCATION

INTRODUCTION

All Member countries have witnessed in recent years a shift from a selective to a more open system of higher education. In some countries this has been accompanied by a growing conviction that the whole post-secondary sector of education ought to be reformed and rationalized. It is for this reason that the term "post-secondary" has been invoked to comprehend a wide spectrum of programmes from advanced degree courses to some of the unstructured activities sponsored by adult education agencies.

Until only a few years ago the expansion and reform of post-secondary education was viewed primarily within the framework of university provision. Colleges and universities, it was thought, would have to respond to the drastic increase in demand for places by means of internal adjustment of the curricula and innovations in teaching methods. Alternatively or concurrently, it would be necessary to found an appropriate number of new universities.

In the event, many universities have expanded quite considerably and have diversified their functions, often quite substantially. Moreover, many new universities have been created. Yet the scale of this expansion and diversification has fallen short of both individual and societal demands for more diversified post-secondary education. Accordingly, a variety of so-called "non-traditional" forms of post-secondary education has been created to meet the new and varied needs. Often established on an ad hoc basis, but occasionally related to a more general policy framework, these new forms of post-secondary education are in some countries (e. g. Canada, United Kingdom, United States) expanding more rapidly than the traditional ones. Consequently, this new feature of post-secondary education is becoming an indispensable element in present policy, and it will be necessary for any future policy and planning in education to encompass both the traditional and non-traditional parts of post-secondary education. Furthermore, policy and planning may need to be seen in the perspective of an emerging policy for recurrent education, covering the whole formal post-compulsory education and at least some of the many forms of informal education.

REASONS FOR THE EXPANSION
OF NON-TRADITIONAL POST-SECONDARY EDUCATION

The reasons why traditional institutions have been unable to meet the new demand for post-secondary education are many and varied and not always coherent. The following appear to be the dominant reasons:

i) They are not sufficiently diversified and flexible and thus do not correspond to the increased diversity of the individual demand, especially the growing numbers of adult students.

ii) They have not been able to respond adequately to the development in the labour market towards greater diversity, the requirement of new skills and continuous training.

iii) Their general efficacy has been increasingly questioned by both policy-makers and students.

iv) The unlimited expansion of these institutions based on a general entrance qualification acquired in secondary education has proved very costly for governments to sustain.

v) Many people who desire to pursue post-secondary studies lack the minimum entrance requirements laid down by traditional institutions or are unable to comply with the regulations.

vi) Some policy-makers and many would-be students, in particular adults, now recognize that it should be possible to undertake post-secondary studies on a part-time or recurrent basis instead of attending a traditional institution on a full-time basis in a concentrated way for a period of three or four years.

vii) A greater concern for equal educational opportunity also at the level of post-secondary education has been a strong force behind the new provisions.

MEETING THE NEW DEMAND

The rapidly growing and diversified new demand for post-secondary education has been partially met by:

i) amending the regulations and adopting new methods of instruction in many traditional institutions;

ii) the emergence of new institutions, especially short-cycle institutions, performing new functions. (1)

For the purposes of this paper, both the new methods and the new institutions are designated "non-traditional".

Although it has already become an indispensable element in the provision and policy of post-secondary education, the non-traditional sector is not easy to define. The Commission on Non-Traditional Study (United States) was forced to conclude that "non-traditional study is more an attitude than a system and thus can never be defined except tangentially". (2) The Commission also points out that the range of non-traditional forms is vast:

---

1. See "Towards New Structures of Post-Secondary Education, op. cit.; Short-Cycle Higher Education: A Search for Identity", OECD, Paris, 1973.

2. Commission on Non-Traditional Study, Diversity by Design, Jossey Bass, Inc., New York, 1973.

"Even a partial list of such arrangements and programs discloses the wide variety: consortia of academic departments, special guidance and counselling centers (for women, returning veterans, minority groups, etc.), tutorials, external degrees, examinations as the total measure of an academic degree, independent study, work experience for credit, co-operative education, study abroad, computer-assisted instruction, television courses, radio courses, video-tape, two-way telephone, cable television cassettes, films, modules of study, individual contracts, public service for credit, correspondence courses, weekend or summer or other workshops, mento-student relationships, arrangements with alternate systems. Within each of these organisational as well as academic approaches. "

It is certain that in order to cater for a greatly enlarged and more heterogeneous student population, innovatory post-secondary institutions have developed and adopted new measures. These measures have in particular included:

   i) employing members of staff whose academic qualifications would previously have been considered inadequate;
  ii) employing on part-time contracts instructors engaged in industry and commerce, for example accountants and lawyers;
 iii) broadening the traditional curricula so as to include new subjects and to allow students to study new combinations of subjects;
  iv) introducing new methods of instruction either to complement or to replace traditional methods, for example tuition by correspondence or programmed learning devices;
   v) changing admission regulations, for example by regarding work experience as an alternative to completing the normal period of secondary education;
  vi) acknowledging for the purpose of accreditation periods of study undertaken in other institutions;
 vii) permitting registered students to follow courses away from the institutional campus;
viii) permitting students to study on a part-time basis in the evenings, at weekends, at summer schools or for periodic blocks of full-time attendance;
  ix) using continuous assessment rather than terminal examinations as a means of final accreditation;
   x) co-operating with other institutions in the provision and recognition of courses of instruction.

Many of these new innovations represent attempts to construct "time-free", "space-free" and "age-free" courses carefully tailored to individual learning needs and making the optimum use of all available instructional aids. Such courses are based on the notion of a much more flexible time variable than the academic year, and on the theory that the actual place for study could be at home or at work as well as on a campus and, furthermore, that a student population more diversified in age and experience is of importance. Examples of such programmes are:

- external degree programmes (Australia, Canada, France, United Kingdom, United States);
- open university programmes (Japan, Spain, United Kingdom, United States);
- universities without walls (United States);
- multi-campus programmes (Canada, United States).

A large amount of non-traditional post-secondary education also takes place under non-academic auspices totally outside the formal educational system. Many industrial and commercial firms as well as major public bodies provide an increasing amount of in-service training and career education. For example, in Massachusetts (United States) the right to award education degrees is no longer the exclusive prerogative of colleges and universities: recently a firm was given the right to grant academic degrees of Master of Science in Administration. It is also a well-known fact that many of the large multi-national enterprises spend a considerable amount of resources on internal educational programmes - often of a very high quality. Whether these kinds of educational activities should or could be co-ordinated with other forms of traditional post-secondary education is questionable, but they should perhaps be taken into account in the future planning of the more traditional forms.

SOME ESSENTIAL POLICY IMPLICATIONS
OF THE NEW DEVELOPMENTS

The advancement of new policies for the total post-secondary field is of primary concern to most OECD Member countries. The general concepts around which the new policies are formulated are: greater variety in programmes in order to meet a much more diversified individual demand, and shorter and possibly less expensive programmes. Furthermore, it is beginning to be recognized that a great deal of relevant education takes place outside the formal educational system. The most prominent feature of these new policies has been the establishment of short-cycle institutions (1) of post-secondary education. These, together with other forms of non-traditional post-secondary education, now represent in many Member countries a large and important part of the whole post-secondary field. Its rapid expansion poses many intricate policy questions, but two seem to be outstanding:

- the relationship between the traditional sector and the non-traditional sector;
- the expansion of the non-traditional sector and its relation to adult education and an emerging policy for recurrent education.

As regards the relationship between the non-traditional sector and the traditional sector of education, governments have so far responded in one of three ways:

i) by creating what in the United Kingdom has been called a "binary" system - that is, treating the traditional and non-traditional sectors as separate entities;
ii) by regarding post-secondary education as a totality and creating an integrated, but diversified, system embodying all its institutional manifestations and co-ordinating them as much as possible (e. g. German "Gesamthochschule", Danish University Centre Projects and Swedish "U 68" proposals);
iii) by treating the two sectors as interdependent (e. g. Norway, emphasizing the development of a new network of Regional Colleges and a partial reform of universities with close links between the two; France, with its reform of universities and the foundation of IUTs; some states in the USA and certain provinces in Canada).

1. "Towards New Structures of Post-Secondary Education", op. cit.; Short-Cycle Higher Education: A Search for Identity, op. cit.

Irrespective of the three approaches, there seems to be a gap in prestige between traditional and non-traditional forms, a gap which is wider in most European countries than it is, for example, in North America. At the same time it would be misleading to suppose that there is a strict polarization: on the one hand, the new forms of study are making some impact upon traditional institutions in respect of curricular reform and methods of instruction and, on the other, although the design of new course structures and new methods is undoubtedly the product of much radical thought, each national, state or provincial system of post-secondary education is ultimately built upon existing foundations.

One of the unstated intentions of a policy to establish new forms of post-secondary education was to direct students away from overcrowded universities. This would, in fact, allow the universities to continue exercising their traditional role and maintain their status as high-prestige institutions. However, the problems that have emerged are formidable. In many cases the new institutions strive to gain the same prestige as the "long", traditional institutions by raising standards, stiffening admission conditions and lengthening courses. Students often turn away from the programmes that provide occupational qualifications and prefer those programmes that allow them to transfer to long-cycle institutions. It must be added, however, that in some instances the policy has been successful and some of the new institutions are more popular among students than the conventional ones. The Regional Colleges in Norway are a case in point.

Another crucial issue in the relationship between the two sectors is the question of social selection. The main problem is whether the new policies can handle the selection process in such a way that the drawbacks of the binary system are overcome in a socially acceptable manner. To the extent that policies for developing broader post-secondary structures are intended to direct the flood of students away from the universities, the question must be raised as to how this affects the process of social selection.

Concerning the expansion of the non-traditional sector of post-secondary education and its relation to adult and recurrent education, there has been a tendency to consider the new trends in post-secondary education in isolation from educational trends in general. The problem of this tendency becomes apparent when it is recognized that the recent unprecedented expansion of post-secondary education often has been unrelated to an increasing public commitment to the idea of a system of recurrent education. For policy-makers anxious to start implementing this idea it is not simply a question of formulating schemes for comprehensive post-secondary education but of striving for a still more far-seeking goal, that is, the integration of secondary and post-secondary education into a post-compulsory system based on the notion of a policy for recurrent education.

The concept of recurrent education proposes a concrete framework within which a great part of individual lifelong learning can take place. It differs from the concept of "permanent education" by making the principle of alternation between education and other activities central to the definition. Accordingly, recurrent education is a proposal for a new, alternative educational strategy to reform the array of educational provisions, formal and informal, for young people and adults, at present available. It is a long-term planning strategy and not a proposal for sudden radical change. As its planning includes suggestions for a gradual reorientation of the present towards the future, it has immediate implications for educational policy and innovation at all levels, including the post-secondary level. (1)

1. For a detailed discussion of this concept see: Recurrent Education: A Strategy for Lifelong Learning, op. cit.

While the trends of non-traditional forms of post-secondary education outlined above no doubt contribute to creating favourable conditions for a system of recurrent education, they are not sufficient as they often are not part of the overall restructuring of post-compulsory education, nor are they co-ordinated with related innovations in other social sectors.

While recurrent education has attracted great interest in many Member countries as a possible alternative to the continuous growth of higher education, it is also becoming recognized that the problems in higher education are to a great extent a function of the structures and objectives of secondary education and, consequently, a reorganisation of secondary education is of vital importance to the development of the post-secondary sector towards a system of recurrent education. Hence, the introduction of recurrent education, if it is to be successful, must be part of a wider policy for educational change in which all types and levels are carefully co-ordinated and account is taken of their interaction. Recurrent education will necessitate reforms in curricula and structure, both at the compulsory and post-compulsory education level. It also implies bringing upper secondary and post-secondary education together into one flexible and integrated system. An essential starting point for this reorientation of policies lies in new approaches towards the 16 to 19 age group. Reform of the upper end of secondary school is therefore a crucial issue in order to enable a smoother transition from study to work and to make the choice between leaving the education system or going on to higher education less final. Such a policy would have great impact on the post-secondary sector. It would have to respond to a still larger number of young adults and be able to provide them with a meaningful alternation between work and education.

Current reforms in post-secondary education have also largely taken place without reference to that part of the field which is commonly designated adult education. One reason is that the main emphasis on educational expansion has been directed towards an extension of academic education or vocational training, especially for the young. This neglect of adult education is unwarranted, on two grounds. First, some of the approaches characteristic of adult education could be introduced with advantage into the formal sector. Second, and more important, there is a serious possibility that the opening of access to higher education, removing apparently one social injustice, will create a more glaring injustice by dimming still further the opportunity of advancement for adults who have not profited from a secondary education in the first place. In other words, it is arguable that the provision of secondary education for adults should have priority over post-secondary education for young people. Implicit in a policy of recurrent education is a more careful analysis of the interaction between new forms of supply and demand, especially in the context of equal educational opportunity. If the new forms of study discussed above continue to expand primarily at the post-secondary level, they will not provide equal educational opportunity to the majority of the adults; consequently, within the framework of a policy for recurrent education and existing inter-generational inequalities, new forms of study would also have to be developed below the post-secondary level.

CONCLUSION

A more diversified individual demand and social and technological development both indicate a rapid growth of non-traditional forms of higher education during the coming decade. The effect on and relation to the traditional forms of study are hard to predict. However, whether this relationship will take the form of a binary model or an interdependent or comprehensive model depends to a great extent on the general policy framework and on a deliberate long-term planning for the whole post-compulsory field. Much of the development of new forms of study has been a function of ad hoc solutions and "crisis management" in order to cope with increased enrolments and new individual and societal demands on higher education. What seems to be needed is a new policy framework for the whole post-compulsory sector. Such a framework exists possibly in terms of a policy for recurrent education. It does not give clear-cut answers to all the problems discussed in this paper but provides a conceptual framework for the further development of post-compulsory education.

III

THE STRUCTURE OF STUDIES AND THE PLACE OF RESEARCH IN MASS HIGHER EDUCATION

GENERAL CONSIDERATIONS

This paper is concerned with two related themes of crucial importance to the future development of post-secondary structures in OECD Member countries. Both depend in fact upon certain assumptions as to the most valid means of organising knowledge, of evaluating and accommodating new contributions to knowledge and of transmitting knowledge to new generations. As these issues lie at the very core of the purpose of the educational system it is not surprising that they are profoundly affected by the advent of mass higher education, particularly with regard to the traditional role of the university in developing scientific knowledge and training the higher professions.

The scientist has tended to organise his accumulated understanding into what we call disciplines and to evaluate research in terms of the contribution its results make to issues defined as problematic by his discipline. These disciplines have acquired a social (as well as epistemological) reality, manifest at the levels of scientific societies' journals and (most important here) academic departments. The organisation of what is taught has been forced to correspond to the disciplinary organisation of knowledge, creating graduates in the image of their teachers. The low value placed upon the solutions to problems of external, rather than purely scientific, significance has been transmitted from teacher to student. Little value has been placed upon reflective (synthetic) inquiry or upon the process of doing research, even though these may represent the principal mechanisms by which research contributes to teaching. Thus, the two issues are all the more related in the light of current experiments involving research as a pedagogic device, leading to the view that the organisation of research in an academic institution should not be regarded as sacrosanct and unquestionable but must be appraised in the light of the intellectual and vocational functions of that institution. Policy - towards research, towards teaching - is something for academic institutions as well as for governments. Such policies are becoming urgent because of the current trend towards expansion of higher education at post-graduate level and the need to relate this to changes at the level of undergraduate education. Many governments and institutions are in fact introducing significant such changes in the organisation of studies as a policy instrument for structural reform.

Any higher education policy must be formulated in the light of an extrapolation of current trends (curricular, structural, quantitative) on the one hand, and of the specific goals which it is ultimately desired to attain on the other. Thus, adjustments in policy will be necessary where, when, and to the extent that such extrapolation appears to point to a situation divergent from that desired. It is important that there be no confusion between that which is desired and that which appears probable in the light of existing trends. Clearly, in international comparison the probabilities of one educational system may correspond to the objectives of another, and policies adopted in one country may be of use in achieving the objectives of another if their implications are made explicit. Equally, of course, once their effects are understood the superficial attractiveness of the policies or experiments of others may disappear.

A number of the national trends relevant to consideration of the subject of this paper (e. g. enrolments, the changing social composition of the student body) are well-known or described elsewhere and need not be repeated here. This paper first outlines certain trends in the organisation of academic research, dictated largely by the needs of science itself or of government-for-science but which have had important effects upon the academic system. It then discusses certain experiments (in the organisation of research, in the relation of research to learning and in the organisation of learning) which may be of wider value, and concludes with a more specific analysis of pedagogic and organisational aspects of trends and changes in the structure of studies.

TRENDS IN RESEARCH

Certain trends have been innate in the development of science itself. Research has tended to produce knowledge that is increasingly technical, disciplined and often oriented to the methods of the physical sciences. Knowledge has become increasingly fragmented or differentiated as academic disciplines continue to give rise to a growing number of sub-disciplines. As individual scientists become increasingly specialized, the reintegration of knowledge becomes more and more difficult.

Other trends have been the result of policies adopted, particularly in the finance of research. In recent years an increasing proportion of academic research has been financed not from universities' own funds but by research bodies (e. g. research councils) in response to specific projet applications made by individual scientists. Applications have been evaluated by committees of the scientists' peers and (traditionally at least) in terms of the likely contribution to the development of the discipline. This tendency towards project support has been most marked in the larger OECD Member countries and is at its highest in the United States; in a number of the smaller countries, where research is still largely supported from university funds, it is one focus of current policy. More recently these research councils have departed from their traditional policy of passive response to the requests of university scientists and have sought more actively to influence the development of academic research. Policies have been directed towards the harmonization of research with regional development policy (e. g. in Norway, France); the development of a complementary policy towards post-graduate education (Germany, United Kingdom); the orientation of research towards areas in need of special encouragement, whether for scientific or economic reasons (France, Germany, United Kingdom); and the increase in the effectiveness of research by concentrating it in large centres (e. g. Germany, United Kingdom). More recently in the United States, National Science Foundation policy has been concerned rather with alleviating some of the difficulties which now appear to result from a high dependence upon project support. Some of these difficulties are outlined below. What, indeed, are the effects of substantial project funding upon the academic institution?

Many of its effects have been advantageous. It allows the rapid initiation of new lines of research. It subjects research proposals to the informed scrutiny of experts in the field rather than to the less expert internal political process of the university. Project support, therefore, inhibits the continuation of research which no longer shows promise. It permits the relative allocation of resources to the scientific disciplines to reflect clearly formulated priorities rather than, as was so often the case, to reflect no more than the growth of student numbers in the various academic departments. Project funding has been an effective instrument of innovation in the hands of the science policy-maker.

But, equally, it has had numerous disadvantageous effects, most notably in the United States. It has served increasingly to concentrate research within a limited number of "elite" institutions, thereby creating inter-institutional strains and rivalries and accentuating the staffing problems of the poorer colleges. It has helped to reduce both the quality of undergraduate teaching and its status as a component of the academic role (It has become less and less "respectable" simply to teach). Academic scientists have become more and more "cosmopolitan", owing their loyalty increasingly to their discipline and being less and less concerned with the well-being of the institution which temporarily houses them. The fact that such funds have been disproportionately available in the natural sciences has resulted in the methods of these sciences being aped by other disciplines, in intra-institutional strains and rivalries, and in distortion of the balance of work within universities. Thus the value of an increasing level of project funding must now be questioned from the viewpoint of the academic institution rather than of the science policy-maker. To what extent should institutions of post-secondary education develop in response to priorities which are formulated elsewhere and which are of an essentially non-pedagogic, non-vocational nature? Should they not rather seek to retain (or attain) corporate power over their own development? In part this would entail the internal pre-evaluation of research proposals in the light of institutional criteria. In "elitist" institutions such criteria might appropriately be of a strictly "internalist", scientific kind. But in "mass institutions" they will more frequently take account of the wider responsibilities of the institution. A number of academic institutions (e. g. the British Polytechnics, the Norwegian Regional Colleges) are attempting to impose such corporate values - among which pedagogic and local responsibilities figure prominently - on their research. The formulation of such criteria and their utilization by an institutional research committee is an innovation worthy of general consideration.

There is no reason to suppose that scientific excellence corresponds in any a priori way to pedagogic value. This must be borne in mind in the evaluation of faculty research proposals. But it is a potentially more acute problem at the level of post-graduate training. Here again, scientific needs and considerations have taken precedence in many countries. For example, the support of research students from research grants (as assistants) tends to ensure that whilst their work may contribute to some project of substantial scientific interest, little thought is given to its educational benefits. (By contrast, their wholesale support from educational sources may have the opposite result.)

It is possible to go further than simple evaluation in seeking to realise the full pedagogic potential of research projects. It may be feasible to associate undergraduate students with a faculty research project, or indeed to encourage students to initiate their own projects. A number of experiments in student-initiated-research are in fact being made at the present time, and it is relevant to review their rationale and implications.

STUDENT-INITIATED-RESEARCH

Two of the most thoroughgoing experiments of this kind are to be found in the University Centre of Roskilde (Denmark) and in the University of Bremen (Germany). In the former, students begin with two years of "basic education"; in the latter, education is based on the "project studies". In both cases the attempt to refashion the curriculum was in part stimulated by a socialist critique both of the structure of studies and of the values and structure of the university. In both cases projects for examination are selected by groups of students: an attempt to replace a traditional educational emphasis on competition by a new emphasis on co-operation. In both cases selected projects are likely to be multi-disciplinary: oriented towards the mixture of knowledge and methodologies required for the solution of social, rather than purely scientific, problems. In both cases projects are to be socially relevant. The role of academic staff is largely one of counsellor – to be consulted by students as they require. Formal teaching is kept to a minimum. Moreover, at Roskilde at least, it is intended that faculty research projects - which are to be widely discussed in the institution before their initiation - will be closely related to student projects. It may be said in favour of experiments of this kind that they inculcate values of communality and co-operativeness; they stimulate a high degree of motivation by allowing students substantial control over their own education; and they prepare students for the (problem-solving) tasks which they will ultimately be called upon to perform in employment. In addition, the initiation of projects by students would seem an important stimulus to innovation (pedagogic and organisational), perhaps fulfilling an equal and complementary function to the stimulus provided by externally funded research.

But there are a number of important negative implications. The desire to explore the external world and to control one's own education generally demands a high degree of initial academic motivation. Education based around autonomously chosen problems corresponds to the norms of the basic research community rather than to those of a world in which problems are dictated by extrinsic needs. Finally, the instrumental value of education of this kind is by no means apparent. Its lack of any clearly vocational function is likely to render it distinctly unattractive to working class students. For all of these reasons it has to be seen as a pedagogic device suitable only for an academic elite.

The U.S. National Science Foundation (NSF) seems to have realised this in initiating its own programme of Student-Originated-Studies, in which groups of students may be awarded grants to carry out short research projects conceived by themselves. Since its initiation in 1970 the scheme has been intended for students of high ability "who can demonstrate their readiness to assume increased responsibility for their own educational development". It should "encourage (them) to express in productive ways their concern for the well-being of the United States by applying their scientific and technological expertise to the study of significant social problems". It may be argued that this approach, which seeks out and feeds educational maturity and the exploratory instinct

122

wherever it can be identified (whether in an elitist or non-elitist institution), is the more appropriate in a mass system of post-secondary education. Of course there would be great value in the initiation of a similar scheme by a private foundation, which might be more receptive to radical, action oriented projects than is possible for a government agency.

More recently, the NSF has begun to appreciate the potentially innovative influence which its scheme may exert upon the host institution. It tries therefore to persuade institutions to regard the successful completion of such a project as a significant part of the student's educational development. Such work should therefore be credited towards his degree. This leads to a discussion of issues concerning the structure of studies.

STRUCTURE OF STUDIES:
PEDAGOGIC AND ORGANISATIONAL ASPECTS

The main set of problems concerning the content and structure of studies relates to "the most appropriate sequences and relationships between general and specialized education, between theoretical and practical instruction, and also between formal education and work experiences". (1) It may well be that this is the most crucial issue for the future of higher education and the development of a diversified and integrated post-secondary system because its solution will, in the final analysis, determine the flows of students to and from higher education and their mobility between different educational institutions and between education and employment.

Traditional pedagogy, which is still largely reflected in existing structures, postulated only unilateral relationships and flows, from general to specialized, from abstract and theoretical to practical, and from education to job. Reactions against the exclusive place of this pedagogy have multiplied during the last few years, for a number of reasons. First, because it is based on a rigid division between vocational and work-related education on the one hand, and academic education on the other; secondly, because it makes a development towards recurrent education and a system of alternation between work and study very difficult, if not impossible; and, thirdly, because it implies an educational structure which, even if institutionally diversified, is characterized by fragmentation, disconnection and blind alleys.

The solutions sought in Member countries tend in the first place towards the inclusion of more general and academic courses in vocationally oriented education and, conversely, towards the insertion of vocational courses into academically oriented education.

More elaborate proposals relate to the development of a common core curricula based on the traditional links of established disciplines (e. g. natural sciences, social sciences, humanities, etc.), or on a common theme (e. g. health studies, environment, problem oriented courses). Substantial progress has been made in this respect with university curricula and programmes, particularly in the first two years of university studies. The purpose is to provide education which can be considered as terminal and at the same time to allow students to pursue further studies.

1.   "Towards New Structures of Post-Secondary Education", op. cit. , p. 43.

But much less has been done to link and co-ordinate in a rational way the first cycle of university studies and short-cycle higher education (e. g. medical and allied health studies, engineering and short-cycle technical courses, etc.). This does not mean that short-cycle higher education will or should be made equal (or completely equivalent) to the first stage of long-cycle university studies, but solutions have to be found which will facilitate students' orientation and mobility at a minimum cost in time, thus avoiding irreversible choices and blind alleys in the post-secondary system. All these solutions pose the more fundamental problem, which was central to many reforms in the late sixties, of the conceptual and practical implications of interdisciplinarity (relations between the disciplinary organisation of knowledge and the teaching process) and of the relations between professions. (1) More recently, the development of non-traditional forms of study and the concepts of space-free, time-free education lead towards curricula reforms and structures of studies which encourage student-centred rather than institution-centred higher education.

The feasibility of individualized, unorthodox studies of this kind depends upon a high degree of curricular flexibility. Such a degree of flexibility has been traditionally, and almost uniquely, associated with the American "credit system". The system is based on the assumptions that the curriculum in a field cannot be categorically defined; that the professoriat is not uniquely qualified to determine the content of a degree programme; and that fields of knowledge can be broken down and reassembled (whether by the student himself or by prescription). There has sometimes been a tendency to see in the mere introduction of the credit system the source of all the educational desiderata indicated above. Analysis of the United States' experience shows that this is an exaggerated optimism.

In fact, to assess the value of the American credit system it is necessary to distinguish between its elective and its credit elements. The elective element refers to the freedom of the student to select the individual courses which he will follow in pursuit of his degree. In its traditional form it therefore allowed (perhaps forced) the student himself to design the intellectual structure of his learning. The credit element is essentially a useful administrative device but one founded upon various pedagogic assumptions. One of these is the notion of breakdown and reassembly of knowledge; another is that the extent, or quantity, of learning can be equated with the number of classroom hours of instruction. Credit points are used in the United States both as a common language and as a means of enabling students to capitalize on qualifications obtained in different places and at different times. In recent years the system has undergone certain modifications. The students' complete freedom of selection has been eroded by the widespread introduction of the major (in which certain courses are prescribed, frequently in a predetermined order). Secondly, credit is increasingly allowed for extramural or experiential learning.

If the assumptions upon which the system is based can be accepted, certain rather important benefits follow from its utilization. Students can plan their own "careers" and it becomes easier to alternate periods of work with periods of education. Failure to master a particular topic need not imply that the whole year be repeated; students can repeat the particular course the next year. It becomes easier administratively to integrate short- and long-cycle education in a single institution and it

1. Interdisciplinarity: Problems of Teaching and Research in Universities, CERI/OECD, Paris, 1972.

reduces the costs of transfer. An enormous range of specialized courses may be offered at little institutional cost. Finally, it allows the ready accommodation of experiential learning: this may be student research or, more appropriately for the majority of students, it may be the practical experience of new, professionally relevant situations.

However, it must be recognized that the effective use of the system requires highly efficient computerized management and information systems, as well as guidance and tutoring for students. The psychological effect upon the student of a greatly increased freedom cannot be ignored.

Moreover, there are serious reservations which attach particularly to the pedagogic assumptions upon which the American system is based. To what extent are the majority of students able to obtain a meaningful education under conditions of relative freedom? If the majority of students lack any coherent educational objectives and select courses (perhaps the easiest ones) on an ad hoc basis - does it matter? Does the fragmentation which must follow mean that the institution is offering a therapy rather than an education? Is the danger of imposing a liberal philosophy of great intellectual appeal upon vocationally oriented working class students not as great as that of imposing an academic authoritarianism upon all comers? More recently, the U.S. system has come to be seen as better suited to the needs of training than of more strictly educational objectives. In addition, students seem to become concerned with the accumulation of credit points rather than with the learning which these purport to measure.

The problem which must be faced is that of obtaining the undoubted benefits referred to above within a modular system based upon a coherent pedagogic philosophy. Thus, more recent European experiments, such as the German "Baukastensystem," seek to offer a range of educational modules which are conceived systemically and which may be meaningfully fitted together in a variety of ways. The duration of the total course (long or short), the degree of specialization or professionalization, the balance between different methods of learning (e.g. intramural versus extramural or experiential), all these should be variable according to the needs of the individual student. Thus, the matter of a traditional discipline (e.g. chemistry) may be situated within a variety of suitable contexts (e.g. physical-scientific, social, economic, technological, historical). But, for this to be effective, a much greater understanding of the structures of knowledge is required, as well as teaching staff of very high calibre.

IV

PLANNING AND FINANCE OF
POST-SECONDARY EDUCATION

INTRODUCTION

In all Member countries the last twenty years or so have witnessed a great increase of planning activity in relation to the rapid development of higher education. The nature of this planning activity - particularly its relative degree of prescriptiveness in terms of the setting of objectives and of defining the means and measures for their implementation - and the mechanisms and procedures to which it has given rise, vary from country to country reflecting the particular social and political environment within which it operates. These aspects of the problem have been analysed elsewhere[1] and there would be little purpose in discussing them here. What the present paper proposes is to focus discussion on the central question of costs and finance which for obvious reasons have come to be regarded as the main policy instrument - at central, local and institutional levels - of control in the operation of the system and in the implementation of objectives. The issues involved are presented in part B. They are set against the general background of policy trends, summarized in part A, within which the planning of higher education increasingly takes place.

A.   Background and Trends

Higher education has come to represent an important "growth sector" in society for which policy-making can no longer afford to rely merely on the momentum of trends. One of the essential functions of planning is to provide both a description and a critique of these trends as an aid to the clarification of alternative future policy aims and options. The following main trends, emerging from the analyses presented to the Conference, can thus be suggested as the overall context for policy/planning in higher education:

    i) the continuing quantitative expansion of post-secondary education towards a system of mass higher education seems to be irreversible, even though there may be seasonal fluctuations in its rates of growth;

    ii) the demand for greater equity, in the sense of more proportional social group attendance, will continue to grow and be increasingly felt as a political consideration;

---

1.   Cf. "Planning and Renewal of Post-Secondary Education Systems", internal OECD document, Paris, 1973 (mimeo.).

iii) the increasing diversity of the student body with respect to background and educational needs will be further accentuated by the growing demand for education from adults, calling for the development of new patterns of higher learning;

iv) continuing rise in both unit and total costs and difficulties with regard to employment prospects will tend to act as policy constraints on the forward movement represented by the expansionist trends mentioned above;

v) the strains resulting from the above trends, the growing lack of consensus on the overall objectives of higher education, and the more general political movement towards wider involvement of various social groups in decision-making will accentuate the demand by both students and their teachers for formal participation in broad policy-making and in the conduct of academic work.

The implications of the above trends for overall strategies for the development of higher education are clearly brought out in the concluding chapter of the Secretariat general report to the Conference. (1) They can be summarized under two main considerations:

a) The need to develop a <u>comprehensive strategy</u> in the planning of future structures of post-secondary education encompassing the total post-compulsory education sector, both formal and informal, and closely co-ordinated with public policies in other social and economic sectors. The operative question here will be how to bring about effective diversification of access to higher education in terms of time, space and study, and to establish more flexible relationships between education and professional experience so that learning opportunities can be spread over a longer period in the life-span of the individual in relation to his career development;

b) The need to plan and implement a system of incentives, rewards and other devices necessary to support the promotion and acceptance of change in higher education in the face of established values and social inertia. In practice this will mean the development of appropriate mechanisms and processes for encouraging <u>active participation by all the social groups concerned</u> in the setting of higher education objectives, as well as in the definition of the methods and means for their implementation. It is in this broader context that the debate on cost issues and financial measures suggested below has to be seen.

B.   Cost and Finance of Higher Education

Secretariat analyses on expenditure and enrolment trends in higher education during the sixties show that, taking OECD countries as a whole, expenditure per student year grew at an average annual rate of 9.0%, whereas the GNP price index grew at an average rate of 4.3%. (2)   In real terms, therefore, unit costs in higher education in all OECD countries have been rising on average by almost 5% per year. This has occurred in a period (i.e. during the quarter century preceding 1970) when

1.   Contained in Part One, II, of the present volume.
2.   Cf. Study IV in "Towards Mass Higher Education...", op.cit.

the climate for expansion was favourable and higher education was considered a highly desirable activity from both the economic and the social point of view.

Given the present change in public attitudes towards the growth of higher education, it seems unlikely that both a continuing rise in unit costs and increasing enrolments will be acceptable. If unit costs cannot be brought under control, the tendency will be to limit enrolments. And since this is difficult to achieve because of the resistance to selection, the only way of keeping down overall cost may be a decline in quality and/or a shift to privately financed and organised higher education. For all these reasons it becomes essential for the problem of rising unit costs to be vigorously tackled.

REDUCTION OF UNIT COSTS

Some economists take the view that, given the predominance of labour costs in the form of teachers' salaries, rising unit costs are an inherent feature of the education sector. Whilst this standpoint probably reflects an unduly pessimistic view of the more capital intensive educational alternatives, it has to be admitted that the contribution of new technologies to higher education has so far been disappointing.

To some extent this is due to the conflict between the use of such technologies and the social and human values of higher education, but it may also be due to the virtual non-existence of serious development work on new higher education technologies. Where there has been a serious effort to develop hardware materials and the necessary management structures (e.g. the Open University in the United Kingdom), new technologies appear to be more promising.

Thus an important issue is whether provision exists at present for adequately financed and well-organised development work in the field of higher education. For most countries the answer is clearly a negative one, and this situation must be remedied in view of the growing emphasis on adult and/or recurrent higher education both of which are probably more suited than traditional higher education to technology-based teaching systems.

As the background report points out, (1) a second obstacle to the adoption of new technologies is the vested interest of existing members of staff. This raises many paradoxes, some of which are worthy of discussion. For example, the criteria for promotion in the universities in many countries are based upon research performance. If this is the case, teachers in traditional universities might find it possible to get a better balance between teaching and research functions if time-saving could be effectively used as part of the regular teaching process. Clearly there are some ambiguities here which need consideration.

However, it is difficult to draw conclusions as to the best allocation of effort in higher education institutions between teaching and research activities, partly because "best" is a question of values, partly because of lack of firm evidence on how the effort between research and teaching is actually allocated. Obviously, one possible way of reducing costs is to emphasize the teaching function at the expense of the research function, and this is one of the reasons why the unit costs of non-university higher education institutions are expected to be lower than those of

1. Ibid.

traditional universities. However, this example reveals another of the dilemmas confronting policy makers. Polytechnics, once established, tend to claim "parity of esteem" with the universities in research as well as in teaching. The search for viable methods of separating the research and the teaching role of the staff of higher education institutions remains one of the important policy problems in the financing of higher education. (1)

Other ways of reducing unit costs would be better organisation of teaching in conventional institutions. Work on institutional management undertaken within the OECD Centre for Educational Research and Innovation shows that capital cost reductions of up to 15% could be obtained even within present teaching arrangements by ensuring that classrooms were better utilized. It is probable that even greater reductions would be possible if advantage were taken of possible economies of scale through the restriction of uneconomic course options, possible increase in student/teacher ratios, reduction in drop-outs and increase in the teaching load of staff. All these matters, however, have to be weighed against other educational and professional considerations.

SOURCES OF FINANCE

Total expenditures on higher education have been rising rapidly during the past two decades; however, public expenditure on higher education has been rising even more rapidly. In fact it is fair to say that in most countries the expansion of higher education has been made possible only by the willingness of public authorities to bear an increasing part of the total cost, including that of maintaining students while they are undertaking higher education. Most of the concern about rising unit costs is therefore a concern not with rising costs per se but with the increasing burden these impose upon public budgets and the absence of effective cost controls to ensure that public funds are being well spent.

The search for ways of reducing costs in higher education is often linked to the search for methods of financing it to substitute for, or at least to supplement, finance from the public budget.

There are, broadly speaking, two alternative sources of finance: from the individuals who benefit from higher education directly and from the employers who use the graduates produced by the higher education system. What are the possibilities of increasing the contribution from both these sources?

Whilst the growth of recurrent education and informal training in industry may result in a growing contribution from employers to vocationally oriented higher education, it seems unlikely that employers will make any significant contribution to the general expansion of higher education. This will be particularly the case if the movement towards mass higher education loosens the links between educational qualifications and occupation. Employers feel that they are making their contribution to this development through the general tax system. However, levies on employers for certain kinds of vocational training and specialized postgraduate education deserves closer consideration.

1. One possibility is the use of part-time staff for one or both activities. In the United States, for example, it is common for university teachers to have nine-month contracts. For the remaining three months of the year they are free to do whatever they wish.

The alternative way of channelling private resources into higher education through financial contributions by the students is being actively discussed in several countries, and loan schemes are already in operation in the Scandinavian countries, West Germany, Japan, the United States and Canada. Discussion of the loans issue is usually bedevilled by the fact that the financing of higher education by loans has a number of different implications and can be discussed in several different contexts. Briefly, the case for loans is, first, that it would lead to a gradual transfer of the financial burden from the public sector generally to private individuals and, second, since higher education presents a profitable private investment there is a case in equity for making those who benefit pay. This view is reinforced by the fact that under present, heavily subsidized systems of higher education it is generally the case that most of the benefits go to young people from families that are already well-off. (One of the reasons for this is that secondary education is in general not nearly so well subsidized as higher education.) Furthermore, many economists claim that if a greater proportion of the expenditure of higher education institutions were obtained from student fees (which could be financed by loans), this would lead to greater efficiency in resource allocation both by the institutions, which would have more incentive to provide what their clients wanted, and by the students who would be more likely to face up to the question of what they were really seeking from higher education.

One of the problems with loans is that it would be only after a considerable lapse of time that they could make a significant contribution towards changing the burden of the cost of higher education. Opponents of loans claim that they would make higher education even more inequitable by discouraging poor people from undertaking it. However, no empirical evidence exists to substantiate that claim.

Four further points can be made as a basis for discussion of the loan issue. First, it is often not clear whether loans are being discussed in the context of loans for the finance of higher education or loans for the maintenance of students while they are undergoing higher education. Secondly, the context of the discussion is entirely different in countries such as the United States where only a small proportion of students at present receive grants from public funds, and countries such as the United Kingdom where nearly all students at present receive maintenance grants from the public authorities. In the former case the introduction of a loans scheme can only increase students willingness to undertake higher education, whereas in the latter it is more likely to reduce the demand for higher education. Thirdly, much of the opposition to loans comes from within the higher education sector - partly from those who believe in higher education expansion or have a vested interest in it, and partly from existing students who resist any move to worsen their present financial situation. The fourth point to be made is that there are few people who would claim that the whole of the finance of higher education should be switched from the public to the private sector; what is being discussed is changes in emphasis. In particular, few people would dispute that the part of the expenditure on higher education institutions which is devoted to research activities should be borne predominantly by the public authorities because research is par excellence a public good which will not be carried out at an optimal level if its financing is left to the exigencies of the market place.

REDUCING THE RATE OF GROWTH
OF STUDENT NUMBERS

There are, broadly, three ways in which the growth of student numbers can be curtailed. One is by restricting the number of students who are admitted to higher education institutions (numerus clausus). The other is by reducing the average length of study of students while they are in higher education (short-cycle institutions, reduction of repeating, etc.). The third way is to use financial instruments to regulate the supply of new entrants or the number of applicants. Since financial instruments are in fact widely used to regulate demand and supply generally, such a proposal may be well worth consideration.

In some countries, imposing restrictions on the number of places seems to be an acceptable way of limiting higher education expenditure. But, even when such restrictions are not accepted generally, there are serious problems in faculties such as medicine and engineering which have particularly high costs and whose graduates enter a narrow range of occupations.

In several Member countries, for example Canada, the United States, Sweden and the United Kingdom, there is evidence of a decline in the growth rate of student demand for higher education. Whatever the reasons for this, and it is probably not unrelated to the current graduate employment situation, it will lessen the need for an overall policy of numerus clausus.

Policies to reduce the average length of study are being considered in many OECD countries. In countries like Germany, Holland and the Scandinavian area, where courses are particularly long, attempts are being made to encourage students to take their degree within a shorter period. In France and the United Kingdom specific proposals have been made for the introduction of a two-year cycle of higher education as an alternative to the traditional three- or four-year first degree, and in others there are proposals to restrain the growth of postgraduate education.

It may be that one of the solutions to this dilemma is a fairly short two- or three-year period of general higher education for a large proportion of the population, followed by an intensive period of specialist vocational training for those who require it. The finance of the latter could be borne largely by students or by their employers. These periods of initial training could be supplemented by periods of retraining throughout working life, in accordance with the concept of recurrent education. However, before there can be substantial policy changes it is necessary to balance the economic benefits against possible "quality" losses. As elsewhere, issues of efficient resource allocation and cost reduction cannot be considered except in the context of the aims and objectives of higher education and the technologies (in the broadest sense) currently available for achieving these objectives.

Part Three

CONCLUSIONS

I

SUMMARY REPORT
BY THE GENERAL RAPPORTEUR

William Taylor

University of Bristol
United Kingdom

1. INTRODUCTION

A common characteristic of the reports and resolutions of educational gatherings is the claim that the "needs" or "demands" of a particular situation call for a series of radical measures, which are then comprehensively listed. Such measures, it is claimed, will inter alia encourage diversity, flexibility, openness, equality, co-operation, communication, innovation, participation and integration. There is usually no difficulty in securing agreement as to the importance of these desiderata. Even the most soured participant is unlikely publically to opt for closure, inequality, non-co-operation, non-communication, reaction, authoritarianism and fragmentation. But it is one thing to agree upon a list of measures that appear to be consistent with such desiderata. It is quite another to make the necessary choices among such measures and, often within unpropitious political, financial and organisational climates, to implement these choices in such a way as to achieve the goals they are intended to serve. What hope is there that international dialogue on a subject such as post-secondary education will improve the likelihood of wise choices being made? There are seven main factors that support such a hope.

First, there is the stimulus to generate as much relevant information as possible, not only about the operation of one's own system but also that of other nations.

Second, there is the chance to learn more about the available techniques - demographic, statistical, occupational, analytical, organisational, managerial, pedagogic, evaluative - that may be used in designing and working an educational system.

Third, there is the opportunity to gain from the experience of those in other systems that have introduced new structures or stimulated new kinds of educational process, and to apply the lessons of this experience to national policy-making.

Fourth, there is encouragement fully to recognize the international character and effects of knowledge created and disseminated by universities, colleges and research institutions. Social and philosophical ideas, economic doctrines, psychological theories, scientific discoveries, technological innovations, cannot be confined within their national boundaries and frequently have major long-term consequences for the life of nations and the development of cultures.

Fifth, there is a possibility of contributing to the emergence and formulation of new concepts such as quantitative planning and recurrent education, and of benefiting from dialogue with those who participate as members of delegations and at the invitation of the Secretariat.

Sixth, there is the value of supporting international initiatives, from one-off seminars on specialist topics, exchange schemes for students and academics, co-operative research and development activities, to the creation of multi-national institutions for specific purposes.

The direct implication of all this for national decision-making is necessarily limited. The indirect influence on the way in which problems are defined and solutions conceived, on the formulation of educational objectives, on the approach to system and institutional planning that policy makers and administrators adopt, has been and will continue to be considerable. Over the years the OECD has provided large quantities of information which would otherwise be unavailable, has furnished opportunities for the discussion of techniques and the exchange of experience, has done much to identify trends and tendencies, to seek out and make available relevant knowledge and to contribute to the emergence and refinement of new concepts, and has initiated a wide range of international activities. The Organisation has performed for countries outside the United States many of the functions in the field of higher education that within the United States have been undertaken by the Carnegie Commission. Over a period of six years, ending in 1973, the Commission sponsored studies that resulted in the issue of over one hundred titles, embodying more than three hundred and fifty specific recommendations. In his statement to the present Conference on the work of the Commission, David Henry emphasized

"In spite of the wealth of information about higher education contained in the publications of the Commission, the purpose was not to provide an encyclopeadia; rather the design was to bring available knowledge to bear upon real problems and real issues and to make recommendations for future development."

Bringing available knowledge to bear upon real problems requires more than information; it demands a conceptual framework by means of which the available data can be ordered and its relevance determined, and which suggests some of the criteria that might be applied in the interpretation of this data. Hence the importance of Martin Trow's call for a common language, without which "all dissolves into a welter of detail and anecdote about Professor A, Director B, Minister C and about 100 universities and 1,000 faculties and millions of students". Trow argued that, as a minimum, such a language should permit the identification of shared problems, do justice to both what is common and what is unique, incorporate some sense of the pattern of historical development of higher education in Western societies, yield clues concerning the underlying forces related to present and future developments, and make clear how changes in one area and efforts to deal with single problems have consequences elsewhere - in other words, provide a systems perspective.

Abraham Flexner argued in his classic study Universities, American, British, German:

"Between the student of political and social problems and the journalist, industrialist, merchant, viceroy, member of Parliament or Congress, there is a gap which the university cannot fill, which society must fill in some other way."

This gap still exists, more than forty years after Flexner wrote these words. During this time many attempts have been made to bridge it. The universities themselves have changed, placing greater stress upon service functions and professional education. New kinds of higher education institution have been created, with a stress upon teaching and the forging of links with industry and commerce. Both nationally and internationally, there have been efforts to bring together representatives of the various groups concerned with developments in particular sectors of society. Given the growing specialization of role and language characteristic of the social organisation of developed countries, such efforts are today more than ever necessary. International conferences enable politicians, administrators and academics from many countries to meet, to become aware of both similarities and differences in their viewpoints, and to do something towards working out the shared language and understanding essential to the fostering of a systems perspective within which the costs and implications of policy decisions can be better understood. Discussion across the language barriers of both nations and specialities is an essential element in dealing with the problem so clearly perceived by Flexner. On the subject of post-secondary education, such discussion, informed both by newly collected data and by the ideas of some of the foremost scholars in the field, is what was offered by the 1973 OECD Conference.

2. PROBLEMS AND PROSPECTS

In terms of the speed and scale of its expansion, the costs to which it gives rise, and its importance for economic, social and cultural well-being, post-secondary education is a major policy concern for Member governments of OECD. Analyses of how in less than two decades over-all enrolments in universities, polytechnics, specialized vocational schools, technical colleges and adult education establishments have doubled and re-doubled, and forecasts of slower but continued growth in the decade ahead, already documented in OECD publications, were confirmed and refined in the papers produced for the Conference. The costs of such expansion, initially carried on the larger educational budgets that went with a period of rapid economic growth, are imposing felt burdens on public finance and meeting competition from other areas of educational and social provision. (It has been estimated that the cost of providing one year of university level study is ten times that of providing a year's education for a child of primary school age.) With a broadening of the basis of educational objectives, and a lack of clear-cut evidence linking particular kinds of educational provision and economic growth, earlier interest in establishing the economic benefits of post-secondary study has shifted in favour of more sophisticated, if necessarily less easily quantifiable, analyses of how the work of universities and colleges interacts with the political and social life of the communities and societies which they serve, and how the education the individual receives from these institutions affects not merely his occupational choices and destination but his style of life and cultural participation.

The Conference on New Structures of Post-Secondary Education reflected all these concerns. It marked the culmination of two years' work by the Secretariat and by specialist consultants, the results of which were circulated in various discussion papers, reports, statistical summaries and other documentary material. The quantity, quality and technical detail of this material pointed up what is becoming a real problem in international discussions of post-secondary education. The declarations of the Council of OECD and of the 1970 Educational Growth Conference(1) concerning the need for a broader spectrum of educational and social objectives has had the effect of widening perspectives, but has also emphasized the danger that discussions may, as a consequence, become somewhat general and diffuse. For so long as we are dealing with broad general ideas the lack of an agreed conceptual or methodo-

1. Educational Policies for the 1970's - General Report, Conference on Policies for Educational Growth, OECD, Paris, 1971.

logical paradigm by which to order and interpret the mass of available data about the development of systems does not constitute too great a problem. But weaknesses soon become apparent when efforts are made to refine these ideas, to consider how they might be implemented and to estimate the social, political and educational costs to which they give rise. The Conference proceedings made clear that there remain considerable areas of disagreement over the definition of post-secondary education, of universal access, of what is entailed by selection, the implementation of policies based upon numerus clausus, and about the curricular and pedagogic assumptions that underlie non-traditional forms of post-secondary provision.

All this underlined Martin Trow's plea for attention to be given to the development of a common language by means of which international discussion in depth might be facilitated. Short of a retreat into the shared but essentially narrow language of particular specialisms, it will be some time before Trow's aim is achieved. The Conference sessions suggested some of the ways in which progress might be made in this direction. They focussed attention upon a number of processes and principles and problems common to many countries, which must feature on the agenda of international consideration if we are to succeed in moving from slogans to analysis, in giving more attention to problems of operationalizing and implementing general principles, and in understanding better the political and social contexts that facilitate or inhibit desired educational reforms.

As they emerged in the background documents, in plenary sessions and working groups, the chief preoccupations of the Conference can be summarized in a single question. In planning new structures and responding to pressures and proposals emerging from within existing systems, how can societies reconcile, on the one hand, the need for institutional diversity and differentiation of programmes occasioned by widened access and new relationships between post-secondary education and employment, with, on the other, the need to maintain and enhance the values of scholarship and science, all within a politically sensitive context of limited resources, demands for greater public accountability and a press towards greater democratization?

To tackle these issues properly requires a sufficiently comprehensive view of what the system of post-secondary education includes and what it excludes. The boundaries are difficult to draw. The Secretariat general report of overall issues interpreted them widely.

"... a new articulation between upper secondary and post-secondary education becomes an issue of extreme importance calling for the development of a coherent system of "post-compulsory" education covering all forms of educational activity after the end of compulsory schooling, one which would include upper secondary education as well as post-secondary, higher and university education proper. Such an approach is also a sine qua non for the progressive generalization of any system of lifelong or recurrent education. "(1)

Bowman and Anderson, in their background paper on the American experience of mass higher education, drew attention to U.S. estimates that suggest that the work of formal educational organisations accounts for only half the total "learning force", the rest falling to a variety of proprietary and anti-poverty agencies, TV and correspondence, industrial concerns and the military. (2) In his address to the Conference,

1. Part One, II, of the present volume.
2. M.J. Bowman and C.A. Anderson, "Mass Higher Education: Some Perspectives from Experience in the United States", OECD Document, Paris, 1974.

Douglas Wright called for recognition of the potential of libraries, museums, art galleries, and "similar institutions as important participants in the learning system".

Clearly it is necessary to recognize the enormous range and scope of the activities that might reasonably be included within the purview of post-secondary education. It is important to take as many of these as possible into account in devising new structures and developing new practices. But it seems doubtful if all this activity can ever be - should ever be - subjected to a single comprehensive planning process and brought under any form of unitary control. Thus one can only go so far in agreeing with the Secretariat about the need to consider "as an interrelated whole all formal education and all education-work combinations between the end of compulsory schooling and graduate education, including evening courses for adults". Such a viewpoint may be needed for purposes of analysis, but it is unlikely to be the basis of an effective policy. To claim too much in this respect is to invite criticisms of the kind referred to in Ernest Palola's paper:(1)

> "... higher education planning and system renewal are ... highly dependent upon the existence of a broad base of support among elected politicians, public officials, institutional administrators, faculty and students ... A new strategy now seems necessary ... that consciously and carefully develops political alliances, and bases of commitment for planning and change ... a plan that does not provide politically valid solutions for critical problems is no plan at all but an exercise in mental gymnastics."

Comprehensive analysis contributes to comprehensive planning, not by providing blueprints for implementation by centralized agencies or proposing unitary control, but by helping to develop among those concerned a shared awareness of the complex inter-relationships that characterize educational systems. Despite the fashionability of confrontation, it is only by such awareness and the mutual understanding that flows from it that there can be achieved that measure of consensus that is needed to make plans workable. It is in just these respects that the work of such bodies as OECD is beneficial and the documentation and discussion associated with a major conference so important.

3. OPPORTUNITY AND ACCESS

The broadened basis of discussion on post-secondary education was nowhere more clear than in the Conference treatment of accessibility to education and employment. Hitherto there has been a tendency for attention to be focussed on the index of how far different social strata (generally measured by the occupation of students' fathers) are over or under represented in post-secondary institutions in relation to their numbers in the population at large. Secretariat figures showed that in the past decade there has in many countries been a perceptible increase in the proportion of students drawn from working class backgrounds. But changes in thinking about accessibility were reflected in the considerable interest displayed in indices other than social class. The post-secondary

1. "Planning and Renewal of Post-Secondary Education Systems", internal OECD document, Paris, 1973. (mimeo.)

opportunities for women, ethnic, cultural and religious minorities, rural youth, and members of older age groups all received attention. Concern was also shown regarding the way in which individuals from different groups and strata are differentially distributed between institutions, especially the tendency in many countries for short-cycle courses to recruit a larger proportion of the less advantaged. A desire to analyse the wider implications of a commitment to open access or to the introduction of numerus clausus appeared and it was recognized that selection in one form or another was inevitable. There were indications that "selection by failure", in addition to being both expensive and wasteful, may not be as politically acceptable as was once the case. Finally, there was sympathy for Trow's argument "against the somewhat casual and rather fashionable egalitarianism which does not confront its costs and consequences for other educational values that also deserve to be defended".

None of this should be taken to imply any lack of commitment to the principle of improving equality of educational opportunity. But it corresponds to a now widespread realization that such improvement is both difficult to accomplish and beyond the capacity of educational policies alone. It also showed that the Conference was prepared to face the question "equality for whom?" The improvement of opportunity now means much more than increasing the proportion of students drawn from lower status families. We have to explore the nature and incidence of the barriers that restrict opportunity, and devise the kinds of financial and educational measures best calculated to improve motivation and performance. Questions of access cannot meaningfully be separated from questions about the structure and organisation of studies, and their relevance to the perceived needs of possible clientele. Bowman and Anderson saw four main issues running through United States' discussions of these problems:

"a) How should we formulate the idea of democratization of educational opportunity, and are we coming closer to attaining it?

"b) To what degree is there an inherent tension between quality in higher education and its democratization - and what really is "quality"?

"c) Which new fields of study should be added to those now available in universities and in what ways should we change the training for occupations that long has served and been served by higher education?

"d) What should be the prime goals of higher education, and what spectrum of functions should universities seek to perform? "

But if the United States has long since moved from elite to mass post-secondary education, and was now in some states on the threshold of universal provision, was this the path that other Member governments saw themselves as following?

The demand for mass post-secondary education has been shown to be heavily dependent upon a high secondary completion rate. Young people who remain in school until 18 tend to go on to some form of university or college education. The Secretariat documents showed that some European countries are rapidly developing courses and institutions that have the characteristics of mass post-secondary education, but without as yet providing a full secondary education to age 18 for more than a minority of their youth. Furthermore, only a few countries outside North America and Japan are at present planning full-time post-secondary provision for more than a minority of the relevant age groups, but plans are going rapidly ahead to augment opportunities, sometimes by non-traditional methods, for those already in the work force and for adults. Mass post-secondary education has many faces. The proportion of 18 year olds who move directly from school to college or university is not the only index by means of which progress towards it may be measured.

An aspect of the problem of access that received rather little attention in the background documents and in the discussions was the provision of guidance and counselling by means of which intending students might be advised as to courses best suited to their needs and interests. That this is an important issue in many countries was underlined by the statement prepared by Beswick, Selby-Smith and Harman on the Australian situation. (1)   According to these authors

"... the knowledge available to students to help them to make a wise choice in the light of personal preferences, course requirements, employment prospects and changing trends is seriously inadequate. The value judgement that in the last resort the choice should rest with the student is widely accepted in Australian society, but there is considerable resentment at the ignorance in which these important choices have to be made by individuals and a strong desire for improved information services to be made available."

There are plenty of indications that such problems exist elsewhere than in Australia. Any system of guidance runs the risk of being seen as a restriction of student choice and a means of channelling the flow of demand to conform with the existing scale and variety of provision. But the contrary risks of uninformed choices and unreal expectations may be even greater.

Such choices and expectations seldom relate solely to the educational content of a particular course or programme. Post-secondary education, whatever it may yield by way of cultural enrichment and the enhancement of sensibility, is also seen as furnishing pecuniary advantage. This is amply confirmed by the evidence concerning the life-time earnings of college and university graduates in relation to those of workers who terminate their full-time education at earlier stages. When only a small proportion of an age group entered post-secondary education, such advantages could to a great extent be taken for granted. Many students lacked a clear perception of career goals and intentions not because their degrees and diplomas did not give them access to advantageous occupational and social positions, but because, given a reasonable degree of application and effort, such advantages were seen as assured. The apparently more materialistic outlook of students today is a consequence of the more complex pattern of relationships between education and employment that accompanies the extension of post-secondary opportunities to larger proportions of the population. This complexity calls for greater refinement or analyses of such problems as "graduate unemployment", the spectre of which has stalked the corridors of many ministries in recent years. Fears of such unemployment have played a part in what Kjell Eide in his introduction to one of the plenary sessions referred to as "the general tendency to attach less political priority to education, and to higher education in particular". They have been among the factors that have contributed to the slowing down of post-secondary expansion in many countries since 1968. They have influenced student choice of courses and been an element in the falling off in demand that some countries (e.g. Sweden) have experienced in more recent years. The political potential of such fears is undeniable. Yet several of the papers placed before the Conference, particularly that by Bowman and Anderson and the extracts from a

1. D.G. Beswick, C. Selby-Smith, G.S. Harman, "Financing, Control and Co-ordination of Post-Secondary Education in Australia", OECD internal document, Paris, 1973 (mimeo).

recent Carnegie Commission report, (1) suggest that caution is needed in evaluating changes in the employment opportunities open to graduates of universities and colleges. The effects of short-term economic fluctuations must be distinguished from long-term structural trends. It is difficult to get very excited about five per cent graduate unemployment when one knows that in the country concerned the proportion of secondary school-leavers who are out of work is twice or three times that figure. The structural issues are even more difficult to disentangle. In the United States the Carnegie Commission suggest that the problem can be seen as one of jobs that are educationally upgraded in that they recruit better educated personnel, or of persons who are occupationally downgraded in that they have to enter employment that is below their level of capacity. Even in the United States, where the proportion of college graduates in the labour force is already high, there seems to be scope for considerable educational upgrading of occupations. Bowman and Anderson underline the fact that the recruitment of better educated staff tends frequently to change the nature of the job such recruits are asked to perform. The Carnegie Commission argues that the United States is far away from the situation in India and Egypt and some other countries where large numbers of frustrated and under-employed graduates contribute more to political instability than to the growth of the GNP. But it needs to be borne in mind that the United States context is one of great flexibility of expectation and of a greater variety of "acceptable" employment than that of some European countries. There seems little doubt that if structural difficulties are to be avoided, greater occupational adaptability needs to be generated on the part of employers and the state as well as students. Such adaptability is helped by the existence of a pluralist pattern of awards and of courses, and by the provision of opportunities, on the recurrent principle, for men and women to return to higher education after a period of employment, either on a part-time or full-time basis.

Adaptability is also facilitated by the possibility of genuine competition for high status jobs from those who come up by unorthodox routes: who have entered higher education at a late stage or obtained their degree or diploma by means of non-traditional study. The actual proportion of posts filled in this way is less important than the existence of a sense that genuine opportunities exist, that the possibility of contracting in to post-secondary education is always present, and that for those who do so there is a real chance of competing successfully with incumbents who entered by more traditional routes. Even those who are unlikely ever to make the effort to obtain higher qualifications or to change their occupational destinies gain from knowing that the opportunity is there if they want it, and suffer from feeling themselves to be occupationally and socially blocked. Improved access is necessary not only to provide avenues for actual movements but also to create a sense of psychological openness, to enhance the individual's sense of freedom and control over his own life. But if access is to be perceived in these terms, it is important that the new kinds of provision by means of which it is enhanced - short-cycle courses, the application of the recurrent principle to education and training, multi-media communication, credit systems, opportunities for mature entrants to courses and careers - should be seen as more than mere relief roads to the existing main routes. It is for this reason that the Conference next turned its attention to all that goes under the heading of "non-traditional forms of study in post-secondary education".

1. A Digest and Index of Reports and Recommendations, Carnegie Commission on Higher Education, December 1968-June 1972, Berkeley, California.

4. NON-TRADITIONAL FORMS

Of all the discussion themes with which the Conference was concerned, this presented the greatest difficulties of definition, not because of any lack of schemes to outline and problems to argue about but because the range of plans and experiments and on-going programmes in Member countries presents a positive embarras du choix. But it is hard to draw a line at what can and what cannot reasonably be included under "non-traditional studies". The Secretariat's document reminded participants that the term includes innovation in both institutions and methods. Some of the background papers showed just how diverse these innovations might be. In their paper on the Extended University of the University of California, Gardner and Zelen suggest that by the end of the century the campus may have been transformed by technology into a "learning centre".

> "... which houses a highly mobile population of students and scholars, a small resident population for study mainly at the most advanced levels, a panoply of laboratories for residential research and an integrated network of laboratories, computer, television and other teaching resources designed as much for residential as for off campus study and research; in short, a network of associations, engagements and resources that will permit the student to have the university or college with him at home, at work and at his leisure throughout his lifetime. "(1)

It is a problem to grasp and to map the implications of such an inclusive concept, let alone to submit these implications to critical analysis. The United States Commission on Non-Traditional Study were obliged to admit as much in their recent report, arguing that non-traditional study is "more an attitude than a system, and thus can never be defined except tangentially" and attempting to list some of the arrangements and programmes that might come under such a heading.

> "... consortia of institutions, consortia of academic departments, special guidance and counselling centres (for women, returning veterans, minority groups, etc.), tutorials, external degrees, examinations as the total measure of an academic degree, independent study, work experience for credit, co-operative education, study abroad, computer assisted instruction, television courses, radio courses, video tape, two-way telephone, cable television cassettes, films, modules of study, individual contracts, public service for credit, correspondence courses, week-end or summer or other workshops, mento-student relationships, arrangements with alternate systems. Within each of these types are a number of different styles, processes and organisational as well as academic approaches. "(2)

Multi-national discussion of so varied a list of innovations also raises the difficulty that what has been established long enough to be regarded as traditional in one country can be seen as distinctly non-traditional in another. For example, the elective programmes that are commonplace in the United States would be strikingly out of place in the human-

---

1. D.P. Gardner and Joseph Zelan "A Strategy for Change in Higher Education: The Extended University of the University of California", OECD, Paris, 1973.
2. Commission on Non-Traditional Study, Diversity by Design, Jossey-Bass Inc., New York, 1973.

ities divisions of some of their European counterparts where there is still a stress upon the "organic" nature of the course of studies. As Conference discussion made clear, there is a danger that non-traditional approaches will be seen as largely the prerogative of new types of institutions, usually those concerned with short-cycle courses and with a variety of forms of adult and continuing education. There are in fact plenty of examples of innovations on the part of long-established universities and colleges; in the United Kingdom, for example, these have been documented in a series of reports from a Nuffield Foundation group concerned with the improvement of undergraduate teaching.

Not all the proposals and experiments that qualify for the title non-traditional will prove of enduring value. Nor are even the most worthwhile of the changes taking place in curriculum, in pedagogy and in evaluation likely to be judged successful if their impact is limited to institutions and courses that are on the periphery of the main structures in post-secondary education. The numbers of students involved in such innovatory programmes is not the best index of their long-term influence and effect. Of greater importance is the extent to which students who enrol in such programmes have freely chosen them in preference to the traditional lines, the extent to which those responsible for the programme are comparable in qualifications and scholarship to faculty members elsewhere, and the opportunities that the graduates of such programmes have for entering high status employment and careers. The worst fate of the "time free,""age free"and"space free" higher education contemplated in some futuristic forecasts would be for it to be confined to low status institutions recruiting students unable to secure entry elsewhere. It is this that gives importance to efforts made in some countries to teach and examine for the award of degrees in non-traditional structures, and to establish non-traditional programmes in association with long-established and prestigious institutions. The roots of nearly all change in teaching, at both post-secondary level and elsewhere, lie (i) in the growth of the body of available knowledge, (ii) in the evolution of ideas concerning what constitutes the most worthwhile and relevant selection of such knowledge for particular purposes and (iii) improvement in our understanding of the ways in which students learn and of their needs and potential. Non-traditional forms reflect mainly the influence of (ii) and (iii). Yet both these are ultimately dependent upon (i), the growth of knowledge, and it is in this respect that the contribution of the universities and research institutions assumes importance. It was on this contribution that the Conference focussed its attention in examining its third theme, the structure of studies and the place of research in post-secondary education.

5.   RESEARCHES AND STUDIES

The relationship between the organisation of knowledge and the institutional structures by means of which it is produced and disseminated raises difficult theoretical issues. The Secretariat's documents and some of the background papers made out a strong case against undue determination of the higher education system by the needs of science policy, exemplified in the work of the high status elite universities which all too often constitute the dominant form towards which, as a consequence of "academic drift", other institutions gravitate. It is argued that there is no necessary connection between the science policy imperatives that tend to be embodied in the organisation and operation of such institutions and the quality and appropriateness of the teaching they provide. Indeed, some of these imperatives may be inimical to the performance of a truly educational role. Of particular note in this respect is the influence of project funding, by means of which government and research councils make funds available in support of research lines which appear to have pay-offs in basic scientific knowledge and/or social and technological applications. Such funding has many benefits. It fosters certain kinds of innovation, sustains a reward and status system that encourages a commitment to high quality scientific endeavour, permits the early termination of work that no longer shows promise, and makes it easier to create centres of excellence in particular fields. Against this, it tends to diminish the time and attention that are given to the performance of basic teaching functions, is vulnerable to fluctuations in government policy and to political disenchantment, causes academics to become increasingly detached from the concerns and development of their own institutions, fosters a division of academic labour which increases the fragmentation of knowledge and the development of specialized methodologies, and further strengthens the position of the elite institutions at the expense of the remainder of the system.

What now is needed, it is suggested, is to counteract these effects by a greater emphasis on "teaching-linked research" and "reflective enquiry", on process rather than product. Such an approach is seen as being consistent with a problem rather than discipline oriented structure of studies. Weingart, in drawing attention to the external structure of relevance and the value of project-based study, emphasizes the radical nature of these proposals. He suggests that such study reform "can only be positive and successful if it takes place in the context of and is guided by a general theory of society". (1)

On the other side are those who stress the importance of what has been labelled "cognitive rationality" as the basis of research efforts in higher education, who fear the effects of mass education on the quality of this research, and who contend that the success of diversified structures and new approaches is dependent upon the maintenance and enhancement of scholarship. In the words of Neil Smelser

"Every probable future trend points in the same direction - that research in higher education faces a long season of downgrading and possibly serious deterioration unless deliberate efforts are made to preserve its status. "(2)

These trends include egalitarianism, which through policies of open access, value added awards, the certification of competence and a stress upon general and vocational education threatens the institutional basis of research; demands for resources for the extension of welfare provisions which compete for the funds available in support of higher education; growing vocationalism on the part of students; the claims of non-elite institutions for privileges such as sabbatical leave, limited teaching hours and research funding that have hitherto been the prerogative of the universities, and the likelihood that these claims can be contained only by a general levelling down of such provision; the extension of centralized control and accountability; institutional and governmental bureaucratization. In respect of this last, Smelser argues

"The formation and effective functioning of faculty organisations are very likely first to exaggerate the very conditions (standardization, external definition of standards of work, standardized reward systems, etc.) that they form in part in order to resist, and second

1. Cf. Study III in Structure of Studies ..., op. cit.
2. Cf. Study II, ibid.

to endanger the principles of the 'calling,' collegiality, individual-
ity and freedom that have been so closely associated with the research complex in higher education. "

We have in this conflict of views elements of the same differences that
the Conference encountered in the discussion of non-traditional forms.
If new modes of organisation and new maps of learning are to be generally institutionalized and accepted they cannot be restricted to the "less
noble" short-cycle and non-university colleges and centres but must
penetrate the organisation of studies and research in the universities
and other status academic settings. Weingart, for example, criticizes
the co-operative model of the Gesamthochschule in which a variety of
institutions retain their existing identity but co-operate together in
teaching and research, on the grounds that it is "above all, an organisational solution which leaves the structures of knowledge and learning
entirely untouched". But such penetration may very well undermine the
very process by means of which new knowledge is produced, evaluated
and made available for use in a variety of scientific, technological and
social contexts.

It is difficult to avoid the impression that the central issues in
this conflict are essentially political and depend on the view that one
chooses to take about the relationship of the structure of knowledge and
the structure of society. Radical ideas stress the problematic character of this relationship, the likelihood that the existing framework of
knowledge in high status institutions both reflects and serves to sustain
a particular form of individualistic, competitive and hierarchical social
organisation. Evolutionary and conservative thinking places great stress
upon the universalistic character of certain of the forms of knowledge,
the importance of these forms to the extension of rationality and for the
continuation of technical and social progress, and their vulnerability
to ill-considered structural and pedagogic reform. As in relation to
most political debates, the outcome in most countries constitutes a balance between revolutionary and conservative ideas. Binary, integrated
co-operative and independent systems alike tend to be characterized by
varying degrees of internal diversity which provides some protection
for the frontier research of the elite university and at the same time
endeavours to find a valued place for the open access, innovatory, "time
free", "space free", "age free" institution or course.
Such a balance is never static. It varies from country to country
and from time to time. Hence the importance of examining in detail
particular aspects of the organisation of studies and research in different
countries with a view to clarifying concepts and learning something from
the experience of others. One such aspect to which the Conference gave
attention was the American academic credit system, the advantages and
drawbacks of which are often quoted when the value of unit based studies
for easier transfer between institutions and the intercalation of periods
of work and study are under discussion. There are many other features
of particular countries' arrangements for the organisation of post-
secondary education that could profitably be examined for the benefit of
others. Of central importance in this respect is the provision that is
made for the planning and finance of post-secondary education, which
completed the quartet of themes on the Conference agenda.

6. PLANNING AND FINANCE

Each of the topics before the Conference presented its special
brand of difficulty for the management and focussing of discussion. How
can accessibility to education and employment be considered without
reference to the principles that control the distribution of status and
rewards within society? How do we define non-traditional studies in a
meaningful way? How do we cope with the important issues of episte-
mology and social theory that underlie any consideration of the structure
of studies and place of research? Planning and finance present a dual
difficulty. On the one hand they exemplify par excellence the essentially
political nature of decision-making. Budgets control the scale and direction of development; politically expressed evaluations control budgets.
Planning implies objectives and control; political decisions determine
which objectives will be legitimated and where and how control will be
exercised. On the other hand, these are subjects around which there
has grown up a highly complex technical vocabulary and range of expertise. Manpower forecasting, cost effectiveness, PPBS, rate of return
analysis, operational research and so on, mainly the province of economists, social psychologists and accountants, have featured prominently
on the agendas of international discussion during recent decades. Is it
possible, in dealing with future structures of post-secondary education,
to do justice at one and the same time to both the political and technical
aspects of planning and finance?
      The Conference tackled this task by looking mainly at where re-
sponsibilities for planning should lie, at the need for a comprehensive
planning strategy (which need not, however, imply a comprehensive
pattern of post-secondary provision), at the desirable degree and kind
of public and professional participation in planning, at how institutional
autonomy and overall planning might be reconciled, at trends in unit
and total costs and possible sources of finance for systems characterized
by mass rather than elite enrolments, and at productivity.
      On this last there was no great optimism that any one of the meas-
ures which over the years have been urged upon planners and administrators was likely to be effective on its own. This is one area where piece-
meal approaches simply do not work. With honourable exceptions, attempts to introduce cost-saving technologies into existing pedagogic
systems have been largely unsuccessful. Some of those most frequently
written and spoken about can be seen as examples of "technological
tokenism", a window dressing that conceals a fundamental conservatism
of practice and procedures. It seems clear that new approaches are
only likely to work when they are conceived as part of a self-conscious
teaching/learning system, in which television, radio, face to face contact,
correspondence, text-books, study guides and the rest take their place
within a total package, as in the case of the British Open University. The
initial capital commitment needed to establish such enterprises is necessarily large. Similarly, whilst proposals to introduce short-cycle courses
and to limit the duration of studies have considerable savings potential in
some countries, these measures are only likely to prove acceptable when
they are seen not as a limitation of opportunity or an offer of "second
best" but as part of an overall pattern of provision that offers plenty of
chances for the later upgrading of the individual's qualifications and educational level. It is in this context that the whole question of student support assumes prominence, not in the familiar form of loans versus grants
but as a means of optimizing possibilities for individuals from varied
backgrounds to pursue systematic post-secondary education at that stage
of life where it can be personally and socially most beneficial.

Continued reference to the essential inter-relatedness of action in the field of post-secondary education, such as has run through this general report and is a prominent feature of the preceding statements, tends to make some administrators and policy makers uneasy. Busy with the resolution of the complexities that arise from the conflicts and competing demands of the various interest groups with which he deals in the so-called real world, the administrator finds it difficult to be sympathetic to the all-encompassing vision of the systems planner. He knows that in reality what we call the "system" of post-secondary education is likely to be a mixture of the traditional and the radically new, the elegant and the ramshackle, of institutions and processes that have been carefully planned and those that have "just growed". Yet to draw a contrast between the world of the planner and the real world, between theory and practice - as some participants seemed inclined to do - is to ignore the fact that all of us, however practical we may believe ourselves to be, are heirs to a great variety of assumptions about the nature of man and of society, about the objectives of educational and social action, about the learning capacities and the individual potential of our fellow men, about institutional frameworks and patterns of accountability and control which should characterize educational provision.

Freedom, pluralism and diversity are more likely to flow from success in clearly articulating and ordering sets of assumptions about complex systems than from ignorance and confusion. As several contributors underlined, the scope and scale of what we are trying to do in post-secondary education today involves possibilities for dysfunctional bureaucratic and centralized control which the absence of planning will do nothing to restrain. Such tendencies, and others identified as being undesirable, must be actively planned against. It has again to be emphasized that comprehensive analysis, attempts to tease out the relationship between trends characteristic of different parts of the system and broader social, political and economic tendencies, and the development of an overall planning strategy, have no necessary implications for unitary control. The Conference discussions reflected a widespread, if not as yet universal recognition that while neither our objectives, nor the systems to which they relate, will ever be completely logical or tidy, there is some point in trying to introduce coherence into our planning and in attempting to conceptualize and to articulate the relationships between the diverse courses, institutions and programmes with which we deal. It is in making this effort that the consideration of concepts such as recurrent education, the transition from elite to mass higher education, accessibility to education and employment, non-traditional forms, the structure of studies and research, and the planning and finance of post-secondary education all have a part to play.

7. CONCLUSION

Planning the future of post-secondary education presents problems that are entirely new. Never before have societies attempted to provide, for a large proportion of their adult populations, education that is personally, occupationally and socially meaningful, relevant and life enhancing.

During the past few years attention has been focussed primarily on the problem of expansion, on providing places for all those who demand some kind of post-secondary education, on devising courses consistent with students' needs and those of the economy, on finding the resources by means of which a larger system might be sustained. The 1973 Conference indicated a subtle but important shift of emphasis. Many countries are moving into a period of mass higher education; a much enlarged proportion of each age group will be undertaking full-time and part-time studies in colleges, polytechnics, specialist vocational schools and universities. The total dynamics of such a mass system are very different from those which characterized former arrangements for the education of a carefully selected elite. The bulk of the student places within such a system are in institutions of very recent origin, the character and identity of which are often still in a fluid state. This fluidity is often masked by the legislative acts or statutory instruments that brought these newcomers on the scene, and by numerous formal statements about their role and their relationships with existing forms. But the present strength and future prospects of an institution are by no means a matter simply of legislation or statutes. In many countries at the present time there is a more or less overt power struggle in progress for the future control of post-secondary education. The outcome of this struggle will determine the eventual shape of the system, the extent and kind of authority exercised within it by central government, by regional and local agencies, by the professions and occupational associations, and by the institutions themselves. There was little explicit reference to this struggle in the papers prepared for the Conference or in contributions from the floor - save for an intervention by Professor Neil Smelser of the United States in the closing session. But many of the topics discussed were evidence of its existence.

To what extent should new non-university institutions participate in research? Should governments intervene to arrest or control the process of "academic drift", as, for example, in the creation of the so-called binary system? What are the consequences of the universities continuing to perform "elite functions" in the total system, both for themselves and for other institutions? Is it proper for governments to use post-secondary education as an instrument of social policy, laying down or recommending conditions of staffing or access, channelling research funding in particular directions? Should the staff of polytechnics and other non-university institutions be paid on the same salary scale as university staff? What would be the effects of equating conditions of work in the various sectors?

It is easy enough to continue a list of such questions. It is on the answers to them that will depend the eventual balance that is achieved between selective and open entry principles, between innovation and tradition, between the power that is exercised by all the various groups that have an interest in the future of post-secondary education. There was a willingness at the Paris Conference to recognize that decisions in one area have important consequences elsewhere, and a desire to analyse what these consequences might be and to evaluate their effects on the achievement of social and educational and economic objectives. Expansion is by no means at an end, as the forecasts and projections included in the Secretariat papers showed. But in the place of the linear thinking associated with efforts to meet a very rapid growth in demand there is now an attempt at a more broadly based "systems thinking", which assesses the costs of particular decisions in more than money terms, weighs up the gains and the losses from trying to integrate existing institutions within new non-traditional structures, analyses the conditions that are favourable and unfavourable to a continued high level of research productivity, tries to achieve a balance and harmonization of objectives and activities within the total system that is consistent not only with the overall development of post-secondary systems, but which takes into account both what comes before, in the primary and secondary schools, and the post-experience opportunities that need to be available in the context of a policy of recurrent educational provision.

The 1973 Conference on Future Structures of Post-Secondary Education testified, first, to the importance that countries attach to global perspectives and comprehensive planning, second, to the extent to which the possibility of resolving common problems is increased by shared discussion and, third, to the important role played by the OECD in disseminating the information, the ideas, and the opportunities that make such discussion possible.

II

GENERAL CONCLUSIONS OF THE CONFERENCE

GENERAL STATEMENT

The OECD Conference on Future Structures of Post-Secondary Education met in Paris from 26th to 29th June 1973. Ministers and senior officials from the OECD Member countries, together with members of the academic community and representatives of employer and employee organisations, took part in both plenary debates and in the discussions of four Working Groups, concerned respectively with Accessibility to Post-Secondary Education and Employment, Non-Traditional Forms of Study, the Structure of Studies and the Place of Research, and the Planning and Finance of Post-Secondary Education. Consideration of these themes, and of the more general issues which are the subject of this summary statement, was based on extensive analysis and documentation prepared by the Secretariat and by invited experts as well as on individual country contributions prepared by the national authorities concerned.

The Conference noted that the initial impact of the growth of post-secondary enrolments that had taken place in the two preceding decades had been largely quantitative - new and larger universities, the creation of more non-university institutions at various levels and an increase in the proportion of graduates in the labour force. It was now widely recognized that, as a consequence of past growth and in order to meet continuing expansionist trends and new objectives in the seventies and eighties, further structural and qualitative reforms of higher education systems are a major priority. Although most countries expect a continuation of the growth of higher education, enrolments are in general unlikely to go on increasing at the same pace as in the last ten years; several countries reported slower rates of increase and even, in one or two cases, stable numbers or an actual decrease. But it is clear that a situation in which a quarter, a third or even more of the immediate post-secondary age groups are undertaking further systematic studies, and in which there is a growing participation of adults in post-work education, calls for education systems that are both larger and more diverse than those of previous periods.

The Conference recognized that each country must necessarily tackle in its own way the problems to which these changes give rise. It is nonetheless important that the particular issues that are common to Member states should be identified and steps be taken to develop a common language which will facilitate the exchange of experience and the discussion of possible solutions. This is all the more important because of the universal applicability of the basic purposes of post-secondary education.

In this context it was agreed that any statement of such purposes should derive basically from the needs of students of all ages, which in turn should guide governments in their allocation and control of resources with a concern to achieve a proper balance between academic freedom and institutional autonomy on the one hand, and individual and social needs and democratic responsiveness on the other. Post-secondary provisions should give students of all ages the best possible opportunity to develop, throughout their lives and as far as they are able and willing, a wide range of attributes and achievements:

First, COMPETENCE, by which is meant the acquisition of specialized knowledge of a discipline or field of professional activity.

Second, a general capacity to place their specialized knowledge in a wider perspective of human understanding by developing the critical and constructive powers of the mind, which can be described as COMPREHENSION.

Third, a familiarity with, and a sensitivity to, the best that has been thought and said in the development of our civilized heritage, which could be summarized as CULTIVATION.

Fourth, the development of those special talents which enable each individual to make his unique contribution to the richness of life, which can be called CREATIVITY.

Fifth, the ability to enter into fruitful, co-operative and constructive relationships with their fellow men and women, which can be defined as COMMUNION.

Lastly, the capacity to apply their knowledge, skills and sympathies to the solution of personal, practical, professional and social problems, which can be summed up as CAPABILITY.

This wide range of student needs and achievements - COMPETENCE, COMPREHENSION, CULTIVATION, CREATIVITY, COMMUNION and CAPABILITY - can best be fulfilled by the provision and progressive development by each nation, in the light of its traditions and resources, of an equally diverse and accessible range of post-secondary institutions. It is by the fullest development of the individual capacities of its members that each nation, through its post-secondary system, can best build its future.

The report Higher Education of the Swedish U 68 Commission and the United Kingdom's White Paper Education: A Framework for Expansion, both of which were considered by the Conference, are but two examples of how Member states are planning, or in the latter case have determined, their policy for the future development of their post-secondary systems. The Conference discussions reflected the fact that the context of such planning is now different from that of the sixties.

- There are the sharpened constraints arising from continuing rises in both unit and total costs, and from the demand being made upon limited resources by other claimants on public expenditure.
- There are the difficulties of adjusting the employment expectations of students to a situation in which the number of professional and high-level job opportunities has not kept pace with increases in enrolments.
- There are problems in achieving an effective consensus on priorities in the objectives of post-secondary education policies.
- There is a variety of points of view concerning the effects that, for example, policies of open access, the introduction of new style modular and unit courses, and the democratization of institutional governance may have upon the quality and values of scholarship and research.
- There is increased awareness of the difficulties involved in implementing a commitment to greater equality of educational op-

portunity, and of the inter-relatedness of educational policy
and a wide variety of social and fiscal measures designed to
break into the cycle of deprivation and to improve the lot of
under-privileged social, cultural and ethnic groups.
- There are problems of reconciling within the new perspective
  of the planning process the broader spectrum of objectives that
  post-secondary education is expected to fulfil in contemporary
  society; these include, in addition to the facilitation of economic
  development, contribution to the quality of life, the solution of
  urban problems and the fostering of social integration.

The Conference agreed that, in such a context, success in meeting
the needs of the seventies and eighties is more likely to be achieved by
the adoption of pluralist patterns of development, of course organisation,
of certification and of links with working life than by the rigid application of any one single basic principle. Such an approach takes into account
the needs for diversification as well as for comprehensive planning, and
agreement on the importance of ideas such as recurrent education (the
systematic alternation of periods of study and of work throughout the
lifetime of the individual) as significant considerations in relation to
which particular innovations may be evaluated.
Within such a diversified and pluralist pattern a crucial set of
questions arises concerning the relationships between and the articulation of courses and programmes at different levels; the content of studies,
the credentials received and the skills and forms of knowledge relevant
to the performance of particular tasks in society; general academic and
specialist technical and professional training; student flows both within
and between institutions; secondary school admission policies, upper
secondary studies, the selection of students and the counselling and guidance services that facilitate appropriate choice. The Conference saw
that the key concepts in developing a workable and acceptable set of such
relationships were flexibility, innovation, co-operation and transferability:

flexibility in, for example, admission requirements whereby those
who have earlier failed to obtain a particular credential are not
permanently debarred from participation in forms of post-secondary education towards which their experience and motivation cause
them to aspire;
innovation in the structure, organisation and content of courses,
and links with the kinds of research and development activity that
both encourage and help to determine the direction of such innovation;
co-operation between institutions over teaching and research and
in the most mutually fruitful allocation of tasks and responsibilities;
transferability of credit for work done in different places and at
different stages of an individual's career, subject always to the
demands of relevance and appropriate standards.

However difficult it may be to indicate the precise ways in which
particular kinds of education provision contribute to economic growth,
to social harmony, to the quality of life, the mutually interactive character of these relationships cannot be denied. The fact that education is
increasingly recognized as an important facet of social policy is reflected in the arrangements that are being made in a number of Member states
for post-secondary developments to be planned with greater relevance to
regional and local needs and circumstances, and with the maximum possible participation of those who are likely to be affected by the proposed
reforms.

Simple categorizations of post-secondary provision which have been useful in the past are unlikely to serve the needs of the next decade. It seems clear that the map of post-secondary education characteristic of the later seventies and the eighties will be very different from that to which we have become accustomed.

It was against this background that the Conference sought to formulate, through its Working Groups, the detailed conclusions given below on its four main themes representing the strategic areas of measures to be taken in the development of future structures of post-secondary education.

ACCESSIBILITY TO POST-SECONDARY EDUCATION AND EMPLOYMENT

The huge expansion of education in OECD Member countries during the fifties and sixties has aimed at meeting the needs of the economy and at providing more equal educational opportunity for the citizens. The difficulties experienced in reaching new groups of students and the existence of a mismatch in some countries between the outflow of graduates and employment possibilities have raised the question of what structural changes are needed in order to make future post-secondary education better serve the needs of individuals in society.

The main force behind the expansion of higher education continues to be individual demand, concurrent with the expansion of secondary education and rising personal and national levels of income. The majority of students in post-secondary education consider their training as a preparation for an occupation. This does not mean, and should not mean, that professional training is the only objective of such education. For this reason, but also because of the impossibility of foreseeing the economic development of a country one or two decades in advance, one cannot and must not expect that the outflow from the educational system will, at any given moment, fit exactly into the employment possibilities. Some members of the Group claimed that the growth of education should be geared essentially to the purposes of liberal education; as a consequence, there would normally be need for a considerable scale of remedial measures to help some of the graduates find jobs in occupations other than those for which they originally prepared.

It would be desirable, however, to have advance knowledge of future trends both in individual demand for education and in employment needs; quantitative as well as functional developments of employment should be considered. In effect, forecasts are an indispensable tool for educational planning, but present experience of both kinds of forecasts shows the necessity of handling them with great care. However, educational planning should not be a mere adaptation to foreseen developments but a conscious effort to further definite goals, with regard to both the distribution of educational resources among individuals and the development of various sectors of production and service in society. This usually implies political choices between various alternatives.

It is thus neither possible nor desirable to plan the capacity of every educational programme so as to correspond to the demand in the labour market; long-term educational planning should rather be concerned with broad sectors of occupationally related educational programmes. Maladjustments between output of the educational system and employment are not always to be attributed to defects in the educational system.

The conditions of quantitative planning have consequences for the structure and content of studies. An educational programme should prepare for a sufficiently broad occupational field, and formal links between education and specific jobs should be avoided as much as possible. In some countries there is a wish to include elements of liberal education in every post-secondary programme. The necessary flexibility and the creation of new alternatives are furthered by a system of study units which can be composed into programmes in various ways; these can be used in a pattern of gradual differentiation.

Some of the difficulties experienced, however, seem to stem from the very long uninterrupted periods of study, in many cases up to the age of 25. Earlier entry into active life may be profitable to individuals in enabling them to discover their strengths and weaknesses and in the interests of their further career development, provided that subsequent educational facilities are made available under such conditions that individuals feel motivated to demand them. In many Member countries, recurrent education is considered to be a useful pattern to meet present problems. Many people think that such a pattern would require occupational preparation in secondary school.

In the view of some members of the Group, every branch of higher education should, irrespective of the interests and objectives of the student, have a professional component. Others were of the opinion that part of post-secondary education should be devoted solely to liberal education. All students should, however, be provided with opportunities to be prepared, not least psychologically, for their first insertion into active life, with due consideration for the particular requirements of modern working life. It was stressed, however, that basic education is also a preparation for future learning and that the full learning capacity of an individual can only be developed if adequate effort is invested on the part of employers in further education, within a working environment which is also satisfying as a learning experience. In many cases, such goals would be furthered by a restructuring of jobs. Furthermore, courses of study should, whenever appropriate and possible, seek to draw upon learning from work experience and to link study to practical experience by means of internships and on-the-job training.

With regard to both employment and the possibilities of study for individuals, it is essential to look upon post-secondary education as part of the total educational system. The problem of equality of educational opportunity relates to the distribution of educational resources among individuals, whether at the pre-primary, primary, secondary, post-secondary or adult level. On the labour market there is no one-to-one correspondence between certain jobs and post-secondary education. If, however, post-secondary education is to serve the needs of growing parts of the adult population and of a rapidly developing economy, it is essential that it is not restricted to traditional courses in universities and similar institutions. The term "post-secondary education" may be less useful in cases where such education does not always require a secondary education as an entrance qualification. In many countries education outside educational institutions is being included in such terms as post-secondary education.

In any case, it was agreed that it was essential that post-secondary education be diversified in its accessibility, content, its pedagogical methods and forms of provision in order to meet the varying needs of student groups and of employment. Examples of interesting developments in this respect are short-cycle technical programmes connected with vocational secondary education, concurrent or parallel education, the British Open University and other schemes discussed in detail by the Working Group on Non-Traditional Forms of Study.

In many Member countries there is grave concern about the fact that the increasing resources for post-secondary education have been very unevenly utilized by various groups in the population. Prior educational experiences have a determining role in the demand for higher education. This is very clearly the case in those countries where only the academic streams of secondary education qualify for post-secondary study and where, by an open admissions policy, every student from such a stream is given the right to higher education. However, the nature of the offerings in higher education also decisively influences the demand.

In most countries, in the student bodies there are inequalities related to social, economic, ethnic or regional background and sex. Measures that would help to level out such differences include changes in the underlying school system, the location, teaching methods and contents of post-secondary education, educational and vocational guidance, and financial aid for studies. In addition, the development of possibilities for people who have left the educational system to return to it through a pattern of recurrent education are of importance; such possibilities would also help to redistribute education over the age groups.

The demand for and the pursuit of studies requires motivation on the part of the student. Motivation is in many cases, but by no means always, tied to future employment prospects; the recruitment of new student groups is thus related to developments on the labour market. Long-term oscillations in the enrolment to open admission sectors may be a disadvantage in this respect.

Formal admission qualifications reflect the purposes of post-secondary education. If post-secondary education is to serve the needs of all groups in society, it follows that it should be accessible through any upper secondary study route and to all adults with work experience or other assessable qualifications. Even if qualifications for admission may be assessed in an open and, at times, informal manner, selection rules in cases where a numerus clausus applies can counteract the underlying intentions. It was pointed out that selection according to ability as conventionally measured, if it is applied as an overriding principle, would result in the concentration of educational resources on certain groups. Whatever the criteria for qualification, it was agreed that among those who qualify there should be no prejudice against particular groups or individuals in their chances for admission. In any event it seems essential that not only school merits but also work experience should count in the selection process.

The Group noted the very close relationships between its own theme and that of the Working Group on the Planning and Finance of Post-Secondary Education. Most OECD countries foresee continuing growth in post-secondary enrolments but at a less rapid rate than in the previous decade. In all countries, planning will involve the setting of priorities within limited resources between education and other sectors and between various kinds of education. Although in some countries priority is being given to establishing certain open admission sectors, no Member country contemplates open admission to all its educational institutions. In other countries it is proposed that present open admission to some faculties of the university be discontinued in view of competing educational needs. Also, experience with the specific educational needs of under-privileged groups tends to show that these will not be satisfied by low-cost mass higher education. Moreover, systems of post-secondary education should actively attempt to overcome low educational motivation which often results from social and economic deprivation.

160

NON-TRADITIONAL FORMS OF STUDY
IN POST-SECONDARY EDUCATION

1. Demand for non-traditional education

The demands made upon the post-secondary system of education change continually: there was a time when the universities strongly resisted the introduction of science and technology into the curriculum, but now a high percentage of university students in all countries seek a "professional" education, and not only in the most "noble" professions. When a high proportion of the age group seek places in post-secondary education the change is not only of degree but of kind, since students seek competence in a wide variety of vocations. Student aspirations themselves determine that post-secondary education must give a preparation for a career. The need for economic growth and the recognition that equality of opportunity includes the opportunity to exercise creativity or entrepreneurial skill point in the same direction.

Where industrial or commercial companies are very small, there is no choice but to make provision for vocational training centrally, which will probably mean in educational establishments. As provision of a wide range of vocational training is not necessarily the task of the universities, alternatives must in that case be established. In any event, the cost of excessive diversification within institutions can be high and can pose problems of management which may be resolved only by tight central (governmental) control.

Nevertheless, it is vital not to educate students for too narrow a career: the danger of vocationalism is that it may put students into closed boxes. The pace of technological and societal change requires an education designed to enable students to change careers as well as to acquire a career. At the same time, we must not lose sight of purely educational objectives - the development of the individual and of his ability to communicate with others, and of his understanding of human society and the relationship of man to nature. In this sense, the subject of study is less important than the new perceptions the student acquires.

Further, we must recognize that student demand might often be for access to the "traditional" form of post-secondary education. Mass higher education must therefore make provision for a wide range of vocational preparation, but must also be broadly based. Similarly, the "recurrent" concept makes vocationalism an imperative, but equally demands a firm educational foundation upon which to build later training. The task is thus not to train students for a specific job but to widen their career and life opportunities, as well as teaching them to live in a technological society.

Vocational training is not the responsibility of the education system or of employers alone, but of both in partnership. Precise manpower forecasting is impossible, and career preparation must therefore be broad. Nevertheless, specific employment experience can be invaluable in guiding a student's choice and enhancing his subsequent job prospects. Thus, the names given to courses may be less important than the experience they embody, as for example on the "sandwich" principle. However, the continuous filling of industrial training places requires careful central planning and very close co-operation between education, employers and trade unions. Part-time courses for those in employment can fulfil a similar function.

It is a mistake to believe that only educationists can identify educational needs. Trade unions, employers, political parties and other organisations all identify new needs. The problem is to ensure that the educational system is sensitive to them and will provide, for example, short as well as long courses, together with courses in diverse geographical locations. It might be necessary to establish machinery to ensure such sensitivity.

With the plurality of demands imposed by mass post-secondary education, it is imperative to identify constraints on meeting them; only then can the form of education be matched to objectives. Thus, if there are groups unable to take advantage of traditional higher education because they are tied to home or work-place, it may be necessary to devise "non-space-bound" systems (like the Open University) to respond to their need for home-based or work-based study. Student-centred diversity need not however require that all institutions be different, as long as the system itself is diverse.

Diversity is demanded equally by the disparity of provision at secondary level which is inevitable in the short-term at least. Post-compulsory education may thus include a remedial function closely articulated with genuine post-secondary functions, providing a second route for those whose early educational experience was deficient. At the same time, we should recognize that many potential students do not enrol because they do not like classrooms; this again imposes a requirement for diversity of educational forms.

Practical measures at post-secondary level can further equality of educational opportunity, for example the diversification of the structure and content of studies, the decentralization of the location of learning (taking education to students in their homes or at work), the development of educational and vocational guidance, as well as fiscal measures.

Every country could with profit study the means of identifying social demand as expressed by individuals and by groups, the relevance of that demand to the present goals of the education system, the pace at which demand and educational goals can be harmonized within a given commitment of resources, and how structures and functions can be devised and allocated within the educational system to ensure that the demand is met.

2.   Characteristics of non-traditional forms of post-secondary education

The dichotomy between traditional and non-traditional forms of education is imprecise. Innovation may include the extension of existing curricula through new modes to new students, devising new curricula, the compression of post-secondary learning through the certification or accreditation of experience, and the certification of competence without formal instruction.

If we are to achieve both programme diversity and student-centred (i. e. individualized learning) diversity, the system must be complex, comprehensive and decentralized in respect of the learning function. The provision of guidance is an essential characteristic of such a system. Nor must the needs of society be forgotten in catering for those of the individual. This imposes an increasing demand for interdisciplinarity, centring education on concrete societal problem areas. New modes of learning - group work, the use of new materials and media - are here as important as new content of studies or curricula.

Further, many superficially innovative institutions remain traditional in the sense that crucial decisions are still taken within the traditional structure of administration or governance: if the system is to be responsive to plural demands, participation of learners and teachers in the decision-making process seems desirable.

162

There are thus several spectra along which the degree of innovation may be measured - the content of studies, the location of learning (centralized, geographically spread, or, even, in the home), openness of access to those lacking formal qualifications, the recognition of experience as a substitute for formal qualifications, openness to all age groups, participatory as opposed to autocratic or bureaucratic decision-making structures, and the provision of educational and vocational counselling.

3.   Relations between traditional and non-traditional forms of post-secondary education

In order to innovate, it may be necessary in some countries to create a dichotomy between the two forms of education before they can be reconciled. Competition can sometimes be essential to successful innovation. New teaching methods can be introduced most readily in special centres, like the Open University or the University Without Walls; they may then "infect" traditional institutions. (Non-educational organisations and their resources - for example, national broadcasting companies - can thus be involved in the education process.) It may in any event be dangerous to overwhelm traditional institutions that are used to slow change with new programmes and new methodologies. In some countries, however, an alternative is to insist upon innovation in existing institutions.

While new institutions are sometimes necessary for a breakthrough into new forms of education, it should be recognized that the cost of innovation is high. Without such recognition new institutions may be under-financed and there may be no genuine competition. Further, only when institutional objectives are clear and their attainment measurable will funds be readily provided. Not only are excessively diverse institutions suspect because they do not adequately meet these two criteria, but it has also proved difficult to expand institutions rapidly and to reform them at the same time, even though in theory expansion should provide the resources for innovation.

Competition can, however, only exist if some objectives are shared. A rigid separation of sectors with quite different objectives would thus not achieve competition. Further, staff would be difficult to recruit for a wholly innovatory sector, and their own previous training and attitudes might rapidly distort its objectives. In any event, a compatible system of accreditation seems necessary if new qualifications are to be acceptable to employers. It may also be found desirable to move towards a common reward system for teaching personnel. If rewards are too disparate, to the disfavour of new forms of education, this might reinforce the tendency to value theory above practice, long above short studies (even in the labour market), and research above teaching.

There was agreement that new institutions innovate more readily, since old institutions sometimes resist both short studies and new demands from the representatives of the labour market or from potential students. Their emphasis on research could harm the suitability of students for the labour market.

Opinions differ, however, on whether it is necessary to create separate sectors, as in a "binary" system. Some countries feel that on the one hand the pull of the traditional university model is too strong to permit innovation within the university sector, and that on the other hand new students, especially working class students, feel uncomfortable in universities. Some argue the desirability of political diversity of control and of a sector which is as responsive to local needs as to national.

On the other hand, in some countries, especially small countries, sectoral duplication may be expensive and create unnecessary administrative problems. It is therefore better to reform the universities, such reform including the foundation of new and innovatory institutions within the university sector. It is argued that this makes possible the most economic use of existing resources, facilitates a desirable integration of universities into the wider society, and avoids the creation of a prestige hierarchy among institutions.

Some participants felt that the status problem is most readily overcome in a "comprehensive" system by calling all institutions universities, others by calling no institutions universities but devising another name. In any event, there was agreement that diversification was imperative, whether within a nominally "binary", "comprehensive" or "unitary" system.

4. Non-traditional forms of study as a focus for the development of recurrent education

Upper secondary and post-secondary education should allow a real choice between continuous further study, and entry into employment with a later return to education. This means that there must be a large number of short courses available to serve as the basis for occupational training, as well as new forms of programmes for those already occupationally active. Here the block-building concept is important: nurses should not have to start de novo in order to become medical laboratory technicians or medical doctors. Programmes should also have more than one terminal stage (exit and re-entry points). The learning function would have to be decentralized. Machinery would be required to ensure sensitivity to the labour market and adequacy of financial support for the occupationally active re-entering education.

While the best base in compulsory education for such a system would lie in the provision of comprehensive secondary education, there might also be advantages in bringing together in single institutions students, both full-time and part-time, who are of post-compulsory age but at a level lower than that of higher education. At every stage, there might be reassessment of potential and further guidance; it is dangerous to create a single, continuous educational escalator.

Curricula might take account of the experience of the adult learner as the base on which he or she could build theoretical knowledge; and the young and the experienced, as well as theoretical and practical studies, could with advantage be mixed within the same institution. While recurrent education can be seen as a long-term strategy, recurrent learning is not a new system but an addition to, or in some countries merely an extension of, existing provision. Further, it is a function of informal modes of self-teaching (mass media, etc.), as well as of formal educational provision.

While progress within hierarchical career structures (craftsman, technician, technologist) is easy to define, it is difficult to facilitate career changes from one defined structure to another or fresh starts.

A further problem lies in the assessment of adult experience. What is not controlled is difficult to assess. It may be helpful, however, to develop means of testing achievement irrespective of formal learning, of categorizing in the curriculum knowledge acquired within a given vocation or profession, and of assessing the competencies required in different forms of employment and the degree to which each of them can be acquired in experiential situations.

A developing tendency is to accept adults with work experience into higher education without the normally required qualification. This trend should be encouraged. Another, more radical proposal is to give credits for work experience related to the studies chosen. Exchange of information about such experiments would be useful.

THE STRUCTURE OF STUDIES AND THE PLACE OF RESEARCH IN MASS HIGHER EDUCATION

The Working Group focussed its discussions first on research and then on the structure of studies, examining the implications for both topics of the advent of mass higher or post-secondary education. The Group based its deliberations on the very useful analysis of the issues as recorded in the Secretariat Discussion Paper on this theme. (1) It expressed its full agreement with this analysis and statement of the problems involved and saw little point in reproducing them in its own conclusions. This Discussion Paper should therefore be regarded as an integral part of the present report, which consequently limits itself to a statement of a number of specific points which were given special consideration during the discussions.

1. Toward a new relationship between research and education

What problems does research confront and what place does it have in the emerging system of mass, and probably increasingly diversified, post-secondary education?

Research is a vital investment much of which underpins the entire educational enterprise both in the long term to generate the new knowledge essential to teaching and in the short term to give vitality to teaching and to involve students in the process of inquiry. However, an over-emphasis on research can distort an educational institution to the detriment of its teaching function. But research should not be down-graded because of an over-reaction to this very real phenomenon. There should also be more contact and interchange between universities and research institutes.

Working out the role of research in higher education depends upon the various criteria - scientific, educational and social - which may predominate at one time or another in the evaluation and selection of projects. These may call for very different modes of organisation and structuring of academic research. Adopting an educational perspective (given that research in the sense of interpreting, synthesizing and integrating data is essential to teaching and yet research and teaching may impose incompatible demands on higher education institutions) the essential problem is that of organising research activities so as to produce maximum benefits for and the least possible disruption of the teaching function. Research may be not only anti-education but even anti-scientific, for example in responding to the latest preoccupations of external funding agencies. The Group urged the funding of research from multiple sources and the formulation of institutional research policies to avoid these problems.

1. See Section III of the "Guidelines for Discussion" in the present volume.

Whilst in mass post-secondary education research remains vital to the teaching function, one must also distinguish between "frontier research" and "reflective inquiry", the former requiring the major equipment and large teams more typically and properly found in universities and research institutes. However, as research is not just the accumulation of knowledge but also, and perhaps more importantly, an "active" approach to teaching, it should in some way pervade all the diverse forms of post-secondary education. Even if recent secondary school graduates can undertake only research that is trivial in its scientific significance, it was generally agreed that research is important at this level, not as a product but as a process, and especially as a foundation for later recurrent education.

Having agreed that research methods and projects are vital to teaching, an important problem is that of the amount of attention a teacher should devote to research, a dilemma made more acute because the teacher/researcher tends to be evaluated on the basis of his research and his success in training yet more researchers. No general rule could be derived. For example, not all university teachers are engaged in truly original research, or indeed are trained in research.

It was recognized that in a diversified system of mass post-secondary education not all teaching staff could be allowed an equal involvement in research (in the sense of advancing or producing new knowledge), even though the academic reward system traditionally puts a premium on research. This also has serious implications for the recruitment of teaching staff. With mass higher education many institutions chiefly need staff who have a commitment to teaching and a proper spirit of inquiry. The problem then arises of recruiting teachers and allowing them to achieve professional satisfaction, given that they are initially trained as researchers and that research has higher prestige and status than teaching. There is no option but to assert that individual emphasis on and success in either teaching or original research should be seen to be equally esteemed.

At the level of the system, one must then ensure that teaching in the mass institutions of post-secondary education (frequently its most rapidly growing sector) reaps the benefits of research without having provision for research on the traditional university scale. It may be possible in these institutions for teachers who have been trained as researchers to continue their research, directing it towards regional and practical problems, and to impart in their teaching the spirit of inquiry characteristic of research activity.

It was indeed proposed that these institutions by such client orientation in research might acquire a special identity and status. There is of course the danger that such teachers would, in time, lose their research capacity if isolated from research centres. One solution might be an interchange of staff between universities and the more teaching oriented institutions (e. g. affiliate universities in Sweden). The establishment of formal co-operative links among different kinds of post-secondary institutions, as in the proposed "Gesamthochschulen", is yet another possible approach.

2.   Research and interdisciplinarity

The question of disciplines and interdisciplinarity arises at two levels, namely research and teaching.

The aims of research are of two kinds: knowledge, through integration into a coherent system represented by science: and social utility, with all its ambiguities and potentials. Within the framework of science, disciplines might represent an appropriate way of classifying categories of phenomena and easy tools for bureaucratic purposes or for the intervention of pressure groups. However, they are often inappropriate for the analysis of real research problems. In active teaching methods the interdisciplinarity which the students will encounter in project study should aim at the two above objectives. Projects concerning environment or urban studies are particularly well adapted for this purpose. It is only after having been applied in this way that interdisciplinarity in research can be analysed.

Practically all professional sectors are multidisciplinary by nature, the only exception being the teaching of a specific discipline. The researcher himself must always take into account the findings and methods of disciplines connected with his field. Post-secondary education must therefore to a large extent be multidisciplinary. Training for traditional professions (medicine, engineering, architecture) are perfect examples in this respect. Consequently, multidisciplinarity should exist at all levels of education. The synthesis of the contributions of different disciplines will be made by the student by means of a real or simulated activity controlled by the educator (clinical work of the future doctor, on-the-job training of the future engineer or architect, etc.). For every major professional sector there must be an analysis of the "spinal cord" of the educational and training requirements which lead to a satisfying professional practice and at the same time to a humanistic culture emanating from the exercise of practical activity within a given sector.

3.   Structure of studies

In the perspective of mass post-secondary education, social integration as well as self-evaluation requires the existence of diplomas which must fulfil a number of conditions. They have to be simple and clear and reflect the level of problems and corresponding knowledge with which the student had to deal over a varying number of years; they have to be adapted to a variety of professional, cultural and personal interests and needs; they must allow for a large measure of student mobility in time and space; they have to be sufficiently flexible to take into account all the student's educational experiences both within and outside formal teaching institutions. In short, diplomas in mass higher education should formalize even what is non-formal.

Although the way in which it has been applied might be criticized, the "credit system" remains the only method which can fulfil these difficult requirements. The term "credit system" signifies, in the first place, an administrative and accounting device which lends itself to a cumulative process over a number of years and facilitates the practice of recurrent education. It thus alone can facilitate diversification of educational experience, substitution of "step-outs" for "drop-outs", and lifelong learning. However, the following dangers will have to be avoided:

a)   exaggerated standardization or normalization, which blocks the system;
b)   modules which are too small, leading to a fragmentation of knowledge or know-how and to superficial educational experience;
c)   random choice based on transient and facile interests;
d)   class-hour accounting, which should be proscribed.

The student should be provided with an orientation and guidance system which will enable him to persist in or to change his original choices and to identify main directions corresponding to his personal development and social integration. The assessment of his knowledge and capabilities should be made in a dynamic and non-mechanic way. Analyses of possible work experiences should be given formal recognition to the extent that they have contributed to his education. The credit system can thus contribute to the personalization of courses. It is desirable that formal institutions assume the responsibility for analysing and according recognition to non-formal educational experience. But in order to maintain a minimum distance between the educational process and the economic system, it would be advisable that education acquired outside the formal system should not be granted automatic recognition.

Special mention should be made of the need to make post-secondary students aware of the existence of information and documentation facilities outside the formal education system (libraries, museums, mass media, etc.), in order to increase their autonomy in relation to the sources of information.

PLANNING, COSTS AND FINANCE

The Working Group took the view that educational planning has a far wider connotation than the somewhat narrow technical activities which sometimes in the past have been called planning; planning requires a constant interaction between the consideration of educational aims and the required resources, and the resources which can be made available to achieve those aims. The aim must be to reconcile the legitimate desire of central authorities to secure the best overall allocation of resources from the viewpoint of society as a whole with the equally legitimate wish of institutions and their individual students and staff to have a degree of freedom and autonomy in the use of these resources. It was in this context, as but one aspect of the whole planning mechanism, that the Group discussed some of the financial issues involved in providing resources for the expanding higher education systems of the seventies.

It was generally agreed that post-secondary education should be so developed as to encourage active participation by all the social groups concerned and to permit easy access and re-entry to individuals to enable them to develop their careers.

Although the position varies considerably from country to country, the discussion focussed on the following assumed common trends: that post-secondary education has been and will continue to be an important growth sector of the participating countries; that there will be increasing attention to the removal of financial and discrimination barriers now standing in the way of economically disadvantaged and minority groups; that opening up post-secondary education to students with a wider diversity of interests, abilities and needs will require a corresponding diversity of forms and patterns of post-secondary training opportunities; that the blending of the commitment of public funds with the continued adherence to the principle of institutional autonomy, in such a manner as to achieve the public purpose of equal educational opportunity, will require governments to move with some alacrity to establish new forms of post-secondary education and will require institutions to devise new ways of responding to the government interest in accountability; that there would appear to be no prospect of seriously reversing or evening out the upward trend of post-secondary education costs but that there are a number of options that should be considered in determining the source of financing needed to support a broadened programme of post-secondary education.

In the light of the above, consideration was given to which combination of central decision-making and decentralized administration would be likely to provide both for the basic facilities when and where they were needed, and for the flexibility of response to the changing aspirations of students and staff and to career opportunities. Views differed, as might be expected from a group drawn from countries with widely varying institutional traditions and levels and forms of educational provision. There was, however, general agreement that provision for the appropriate extent and variety of educational opportunity and experience required repeated discussion between those responsible for the basic political decisions, planners and researchers with responsibility for looking at the whole problem or the whole problem in one defined sector, and appropriate members of the educational institutions. There was also general agreement that within the framework of the plan adopted, the educational institutions should have a very large measure of autonomy as a means of ensuring variety and quality in education.

The size of expenditure is such that public interest in the use of resources, in the costs of different types of institutions and in the seeming usefulness of various types of trained manpower is inevitably strong. There is a danger that the interest in financial economy could induce undue centralization. However, there is a public interest and an educational interest which go beyond economy per se, and there was a discussion on how financial measures could best be adapted to the basic objectives.

Finance is an instrument of policies: it provides command over the resources required to carry out the policies. But it is important to ensure that the method of providing funds is appropriate to the objectives. Line-by-line budget control of institutions by governments or government agencies might be consistent with the provision of variety in post-secondary education but would not be consistent with the desired flexibility of response and innovation. The general view was that the educational plan should provide a framework within which a range of autonomous or largely autonomous educational institutions could most effectively work.

There was a discussion on the possibility that a continuing rise in both unit and total costs, and the doubts expressed in some countries concerning the possibilities of significant graduate unemployment, would strengthen financial constraints. Insofar as staff in post-secondary education institutions share in the productivity gains of the community but do not themselves make significant improvements in productivity, cet. par., unit costs will rise. However, other things tend to vary. In many countries the proportion of students in the most expensive subjects - medicine, engineering, science - has fallen and may fall further, and this tends to restrain the rise in unit costs. Expenditure on staff is the major element in costs, and the Group discussed whether the quality of education (or, where relevant, research) would suffer if the ratio of staff to students were reduced. Given the great differences in ratios between countries, it was not possible to find a single answer to this question though there was a certain degree of confidence that opportunities do exist for some worthwhile economies (and for the disposal of some sacred cows in the process).

In some countries the proportion of GNP devoted to post-secondary education is thought to be approaching a ceiling; in other countries there are plans for a considerable increase. But even in countries where the ceiling has been reached, (real) expenditure on post-secondary education could expand along with (real) increases in GNP. The members of the Group were not, as a whole, disposed to be pessimistic about the prospects for further growth in expenditure on post-secondary education.

Consideration was also given to the methods of financing students. Despite the observations made in the Discussion Paper on the effects on equity and efficiency(1) of various methods of subsidizing students, few members of the Group were prepared to engage in a discussion of the ethical and economic issues involved. Indeed, one of the outstanding features of the Group discussions was the interest shown in understanding what other countries did and their reasons for doing it. The discussions were in fact an aspect of recurrent or, as some prefer, further education, and an experience from which all participants benefited.

1. See Section IV of the "Guidelines for Discussion" in the present volume.

ANNEXES

Annex I

LIST OF DOCUMENTS

In addition to the papers included in the present publication, the series of background reports prepared for the Conference are issued in separate volumes, as follows:

Structure of Studies and Place of Research in Mass Higher Education, OECD, Paris, 1974.

- Study I   :   "New Teaching-Research Relationships in Mass Post-Secondary Education",

                   by Stuart Blume, Consultant to the OECD Secretariat.

- Study II   :   "The Place and Role of Basic Research in the Future Structures of Post-Secondary Education",

                   by Neil Smelser, University of California, USA.

- Study III :   "The Integration of Learning and Research in Mass Higher Education: Towards a New Concept of Science",

                   by Peter Weingart, Universität Bielefeld, Germany.

- Study IV :   "The American Academic Credit System",

                   by Barbara Burn, University of Massachusetts, USA.

Towards Mass Higher Education: Trends, Issues and Dilemmas, OECD, Paris, 1974.

- Study I   :   "Quantitative Trends in Post-Secondary Education in OECD Countries, 1960-1970",

                   by Jean-Pierre Pellegrin, OECD Secretariat.

- Study II   :   "Admission Policies in Post-Secondary Education",

                   by Jean-Pierre Pellegrin, OECD Secretariat.

- Study III :   "New Relations between Post-Secondary Education and Employment",

                   by Eric Esnault and Jean le Pas, OECD Secretariat.

- Study IV :   "The Cost and Finance of Post-Secondary Education",

                   by Olav Magnussen, OECD Secretariat.

Mass Higher Education: Some Perspectives from Experience in the United States,* by C. Arnold Anderson and Mary Jean Bowman, University of Chicago, USA.

    *   Available at OECD Directorate for Social Affairs, Manpower and Education.

A Strategy for Change in Higher Education: The Extended University
of the University of California, *   by David P. Gardner and Joseph
Zelan, University of California, USA.

New Approaches in Post-Secondary Education,* by John Lowe, OECD
Secretariat.

* Available at OECD Directorate for Social Affairs, Manpower and Education.

Annex II

LIST OF PARTICIPANTS

AUSTRALIA

Prof. P. H. Karmel,
Chairman of the Australian Universities Commission

Mr. T. B. Swanson,
Chairman of the Australian Commission
on Advanced Education

Dr. W. Howse,
Director of Technical Education,
Tasmania

Dr. D. S. Anderson,
Head of the Education Research Unit,
Australian National University

Prof. B. Williams,
Vice-Chancellor of Sydney University,
Chairman of the Australian Vice-Chancellor's
Committee

AUSTRIA

Dr. Otruba,
Director,
Federal Ministry for Science and Research

Dr. Höllinger,
Federal Ministry for Science and Research

Dr. Kneucker,
Federal Ministry for Science and Research

Dr. Koweindl,
Director,
Federal Ministry for Education and Art

Dr. Herbert Schwanda,
Federal Ministry of Education and Art

BELGIUM

M. Dethier,
Direction générale de l'enseignement supérieur,
Ministère de l'Education nationale

M. G. Deurinck,
Fondation industrie-université

M. J. van de Vijvere,
Chargé de recherches,
Service de programmation de la politique scientifique
(SPPS)

CANADA

The Hon. James Foster,
Minister of Advanced Education,
Province of Alberta

The Hon. Aileen Daly,
Minister of Education,
British Columbia

Dr. R. F. E. Harvey,
Deputy Minister of Continuing Education,
Saskatchewan

The Hon. Jack Mc Nie,
Minister of Colleges and Universities,
Ontario

Mr. Germain Gauthier
Président,
Conseil des universités,
Québec

The Hon. Allen Sullivan,
Minister of Education,
New Scotland

Mr. R. J. Lachapelle,
Director,
Education Support Branch,
Secretary of State Department,
Ottawa

Observers

Dr. J. G. Parr,
Deputy Minister of Colleges and Universities,
Ontario

Mr. Peter Jenner,
Assistant to the Minister of Advanced Education,
Province of Alberta

DENMARK

Rector, Prof. Thor A. Bak,
University of Copenhagen,
President of the National Planning Council for Higher
Education

DENMARK (cont'd)

Rector, Prof. Jörgen Weibull,
The University Centre of Alborg

Mr. Ernst Goldschmidt,
Head of Division,
Ministry of Education
Member of the Education Committee

Mrs. Lilla Voss,
Assistant Head of Section,
Ministry of Education

Mr. Hans Glendrup,
Head of Section,
Danish Employers' Association

Mr. Bendt Thuesen,
Headmaster,
Ballerup,
Representative of the Danish Trade Unions

FINLAND

Mr. Ulf Sundqvist,
Minister of Education

Mr. Mikko Niemi,
Head of Department,
Ministry of Education

Mrs. Pirkko Mela,
Deputy Head of Department,
Ministry of Education
Member of the Education Committee

Mr. Leevi Melametsä,
Counsellor,
Ministry of Education

Mr. Jaakko Itälä,
General Manager,
Mannerheim League for the Protection of Children

Mr. Jorma Ollila,
Chairman,
Federation of Finnish Student Associations

FRANCE

M. Jacques Limouzy,
Secrétaire d'Etat à l'Education nationale

M. J.-C. Casanova,
Conseiller technique au Cabinet du ministre de l'Education nationale

M. Boulouis,
Président de l'Université de Paris II

M. Picinbono,
Président de l'Université d'Orsay

FRANCE (cont'd)

M. B. Girod de l'Ain,
Professeur associé à l'Université de Paris IX-Dauphine

M. J.-C. Salomon,
Adjoint au Directeur général de l'Enseignement supérieur

M. Casadevall,
Conseiller permanent du Directeur délégué
aux objectifs

M. G. Allain,
Chef du Bureau de l'organisation administrative et
financière des actions spécifiques d'enseignement et
de recherche

M. J.-B. Vaquin,
Bureau de l' organisation administrative et financière
des actions spécifiques d'enseignement et de
recherche

GERMANY

Herr Bundesminister Klaus von Dohnanyi,
Bundesministerium für Bildung
und Wissenschaft

Staatssekretaer Prof. Dr. Jochimsen,
Bundesministerium für Bildung
und Wissenschaft

Reg. Dir. Dr. Hirsch,
Bundesministerium für Bildung
und Wissenschaft

Lt. Reg. Dir. Dr. Braun,
Behörde für Wissenschaft und Kunst

Prof. Dr. Draheim,
Rektor der Universität Karlsruhe

Dr. Dietrich Haak,
Präsident der Fachhochschule,
Hamburg und der Konferenz der
Präsidenten und Rektoren der
Fachhochschulen in der Bundesrepublik

GREECE

Mr. Loukas Arvanitis,
Director General of Higher Education,
Ministry of National Education
Member of the Governing Board of CERI

Mr. Constantine Goudas,
Vice-President of the University
of Patras

IRELAND

Dr. D. F. O' Ceallachāin,
Assistant Chief Inspector,
Department of Education

Mr. Micheal O'Hodhrāin,
Principal Officer,
Department of Education

Prof. Patrick P. Masterson,
Department of Metaphysics,
University College, Dublin

ITALY

Prof. Saverio Avveduto,
Ministero della Pubblica Istruzione

Prof. Gino Martinoli,
National Council for Nuclear Energy

Dottor Luciano Benadusi,
Director,
Education Division,
Institute for Economic Programming,
Ministry of Finance

Mr. Giuseppe Rotundo,
Permanent Delegation of Italy to the OECD

Observer   Mr. L. Pescia,
Centro Studi Investimenti Sociali (CENSIS)

JAPAN

Mr. Kenji Fujita,
Emeritus Professor of Ochanomizu Women's University

Mr. Kiochi Igarashi,
School Supervisor,
Higher Education and Science Bureau,
Ministry of Education

Mr. Katsuya Narita,
Head, Section II (Philosophy of Education),
Research Department I,
National Institute for Educational Research

Mr. Kiyoshi Yamamoto,
First Secretary,
Permanent Delegation of Japan to the OECD

NETHERLANDS

Mr. G. J. Leibrandt,
Deputy Secretary General,
Ministry of Education and Science

179

NETHERLANDS (cont'd)

Mr. C. W. van Seventer,
Ministry of Education and Science

Prof. R. A. de Moor,
Chairman of the Committee for Development of
Scientific Research

Prof. P. Verburg,
Chairman "Informateurs Planning Postsecundair
Onderwijs"

Mr. J. A. M. Weterman,
Director of the Social Workers' College

NEW ZEALAND

Miss Alison J. Pearce,
Counsellor,
Permanent Delegation of New Zealand to the OECD

NORWAY

Mr. Kjell Eide,
Director General,
Department of Research and Planning,
Ministry of Education

Chairman of the Governing Board of the Centre for
Educational Research and Innovation (CERI)

Mr. Arne Kjelberg,
Director,
Department of Higher Education and Scientific Affairs,
Ministry of Education

Mr. Hans Tangerud,
Director,
Regional College of Lillehammer

Mr. Vebjørn Fagernes,
Dean of Studies,
University of Tromsø

Mrs. Ida Yttøi,
Dean of Studies,
University of Trondheim

PORTUGAL

Prof. Vitor Crespo,
Director General,
Higher Education

Prof. Pedro Amaro,
Administrative Reform Secretariat

Mr. Adelino Amaro da Costa,
Deputy Director,
Research and Planning Office

PORTUGAL (cont'd)

> Mr. Cacela Fernandes,
> General Secretariat,
> Ministry of Education

SPAIN

> Mr. Jesus Moneo,
> Head of the Political Science Division,
> Ministry of Education and Science

SWEDEN

> Mr. Lennart Sandgren,
> Under Secretary of the Ministry of Education
>
> Member of the Education Committee
>
> Mr. Hans Löwbeer,
> Chancellor of the Swedish Universities
>
> Member of the Governing Board of CERI
>
> Mr. Gunnar Bergendal,
> Director,
> The 1968 Commission on Education
>
> Prof. Georg Lundgren,
> Director,
> University of Gothenburg
>
> Mr. Dag Klackenberg,
> University of Stockholm
>
> Mr. Lars Tobisson,
> Director,
> The Swedish Confederation of Professional Associations
>
> Mr. Lennart Larsson,
> Director of Studies,
> Swedish Central Organisation of Salaried Employees
> (Tjänstemännens Centralorganisation)
>
> Mrs. Desirée Edmar,
> Head of Section,
> Ministry of Education

SWITZERLAND

> M. M.E. Bollinger,
> Représentant de l'Association suisse pour l'orientation
> universitaire
>
> M. W. Sörensen,
> Professeur à l'Université de Neuchâtel
>
> Mlle. E. Garke,
> Division de la science et de la recherche,
> Section aide aux universités

TURKEY

> Mr. Ilhan Ozdil,
> Counsellor to the Minister,
> Ministry of Education
>
> Member of the Education Committee
>
> Member of the Governing Board of CERI

UNITED KINGDOM

> Sir Toby R. Weaver,
> Deputy Under Secretary of State,
> Department of Education and Science
>
> Dr. H. W. French,
> Senior Chief Inspector,
> Department of Education and Science
>
> General Sir John Hackett,
> Principal,
> King's College, London
>
> Sir Norman Lindop,
> Director,
> The Hatfield Polytechnic
>
> Mr. Joseph Dunning,
> Principal,
> Napier College of Science and Technology
>
> Dr. Michael James,
> Department of Education and Science

UNITED STATES

> Mr. Peter P. Muirhead,
> Deputy Commissioner for Higher Education
>
> Mr. Dale Tillery,
> Professor of Higher Education,
> University of California,
> Berkeley
>
> Mrs. Virgina Smith,
> Director,
> Fund for the Study of Post-Secondary Education,
> Department of Health, Education and Welfare
>
> Mr. William Spady,
> Research Sociologist,
> National Institute for Education,
> Department of Health, Education and Welfare

YUGOSLAVIA

> Mr. Slobodan Unkovic,
> Vice-Dean,
> Faculty of Economics,
> University of Belgrade,
> Serbia

> Mrs. Ana Krajnc
> Professor,
> University of Ljubljana,
> Slovenia

> Mrs. Sonja Saric,
> Institute for Social Research,
> University of Zagreb,
> Croatia

> Mr. Milan Jurina,
> Economic Chamber of Croatia,
> Zagreb, Croatia

COMMISSION OF THE EUROPEAN COMMUNITIES

> Mr. Hywel C. Jones,
> Head of the Division for Education and Youth,
> Directorate-General for Research, Science and
> Education

CHAIRMAN OF THE EDUCATION COMMITTEE OF OECD

> M. Maurice Niveau,
> Recteur,
> Académie de Grenoble,
> France

*
*   *

OBSERVERS

BIAC

> Mr. Folke Halden,
> Director,
> Head of Training Department,
> Swedish Employers' Confederation
> Stckholm

> Chairman, Working Group on Education and Training

> Mr. P.J. Casey,
> Deputy Director,
> Education and Training,
> Confederation of British Industry,
> London

BIAC (cont'd)

M. O. de Cayeux,
Rapporteur général adjoint de la Commission
enseignement-formation,
Conseil national du patronat français,
Paris

COUNCIL OF EUROPE

Mr. Vorbeck
Secretary to the Committee for Higher Education and
Research

Mr. J. Heywood,
Department of Industrial Studies,
University of Liverpool,
(Representing the Committee for Higher Education
and Research)

INTERNATIONAL ASSOCIATION OF UNIVERSITIES

Mr. H. M. R. Keyes,
Secretary General

INTERNATIONAL BANK FOR RECONSTRUCTION AND DEVELOP-
MENT

Mr. Henri Bretaudeau,
European Office

INTERNATIONAL LABOUR OFFICE

Mr. Watson

INTERNATIONAL INSTITUTE FOR EDUCATIONAL PLANNING

Mr. Raymond Poignant,
Director

Mr. Victor Onushkin,
Head, Higher Education Programme

TUAC

Mr. R. Rossi,
Syndicats CISL-Università,
Rome

Mr. H. Hugenholtz,
Member of the Executive Committee,
NVV
Amsterdam

TUAC (cont'd)

  Mr. C. Damen,
  Secrétaire général adjoint,
  Confédération syndicale mondiale des enseignants,
  Bruxelles

  Mr. A. Braconier,
  Secrétaire général,
  Secrétariat professionnel international de l'enseigne-
  ment,
  Bruxelles

  Mr. F. Garrigue,
  Secrétaire général,
  SGEN/CFDT,
  Paris

  Mr. Henri Bernard,
  Secrétaire général de la CSC,
  Paris

  Mr. G. Varagne,
  Secrétaire général adjoint de la CSC,
  Paris

  Mr. D. Hayter,
  Assistant de recherche de la CSC,
  Paris

  Mr. H. Dewez,
  Responsable du Département éducation,
  Confédération des Syndicats chrétiens de Bruxelles

  Mr. B. Thuesen,
  Landsorjanesationen,
  Denmark

  Mr. L. Larsson,
  Tjänstemännens Centralorganisation,
  Sweden

UNESCO

  Mr. J. Herman
  Director of the Division of Higher Education

*
* *

SECRETARIAT

Mr. Emile van Lennep,
Secretary-General

Dr. Alexander King,
Director General,
Directorate for Scientific Affairs

Mr. James R. Gass,
Deputy Director General,
Directorate for Scientific Affairs

Director,
Centre for Educational Research and Innovation

Mr. George S. Papadopoulos,
Deputy for Educational Affairs

*

*   *

CONSULTANTS TO THE SECRETARIAT

Mr. Ladislav Cerych

Mr. Stuart Blume

Mr. Olav Magnussen

Mr. Gareth Williams

*

*   *

Working Groups

Coordinator : Miss Dorotea Furth

Group 1

M. Eric Esnault

M. Jean le Pas

M. Jean-Pierre Pellegrin

Group 2

Mr. Jarl Bengtsson

Mr. Denis Kallen

Mr. John Lowe

Group 3

Mr. Stuart Blume

Mr. Gilbert Caty

Mr. Peter Regan

Group 4

Mr. Angus Maddison

Mr. Olav Magnussen

Mr. Gareth Williams

186

EXPERTS AND AUTHORS OF REPORTS

Prof. C. Arnold Anderson,
University of Chicago,
United States

Prof. R.O. Berdahl,
Professor of Higher Education,
State University of New York at Buffalo,
United States

Prof. Mary Jean Bowman,
Comparative Education Center,
University of Chicago,
United States

Dr. Barbara Burn,
Director,
International Programs,
University of Massachusetts,
United States

Mr. Ricardo Diez Hochleitner,
Counsellor,
Fondación General Mediterránea,
Spain

Mr. J. Embling,
Former Deputy Secretary,
Department of Education and Science,
United Kingdom

Prof. Gerry T. Fowler,
Faculty of Educational Studies,
The Open University,
United Kingdom

Dr. David P. Gardner,
Vice-President,
Extended Academic and Public Service Programs,
University of California (Office of the President),
United States

Dr. David D. Henry,
President Emeritus,
Distinguished Professor of Higher Education,
University of Illinois,
United States

Prof. André Lichnerowicz,
Collège de France
France

Dr. E. Palola,
Assistant Vice-President for Research and Evaluation,
Empire State College,
United States

Prof. René Rémond,
Président de l'Université X-Nanterre,
France

Prof. Neil J. Smelser,
Institute of International Studies,
University of California,
United States

Rapporteur   Prof. William Taylor,
Director,
School of Education,
University of Bristol,
United Kingdom

Prof. Martin Trow,
Graduate School of Public Policy,
University of California,
United States

Prof. Peter Weingart,
Schwehrpunkt für Wissenschaftsforschung bei der
Universität Bielefeld,
Germany

Dr. Douglas Wright,
Deputy Provincial Secretary for Social Development,
Canada

Dr. Joseph Zelan,
Director of Research and Evaluation,
University of California (Office of the President)
United States

OECD SALES AGENTS
DEPOSITAIRES DES PUBLICATIONS DE L'OCDE

ARGENTINA – ARGENTINE
Carlos Hirsch S.R.L.,
Florida 165, BUENOS-AIRES.
☎ 33-1787-2391 Y 30-7122

AUSTRALIA – AUSTRALIE
B.C.N. Agencies Pty, Ltd.,
161 Sturt St., South MELBOURNE, Vic. 3205.
☎ 69.7601
658 Pittwater Road, BROOKVALE NSW 2100.
☎ 938 2267

AUSTRIA – AUTRICHE
Gerold and Co., Graben 31, WIEN 1.
☎ 52.22.35

BELGIUM – BELGIQUE
Librairie des Sciences
Coudenberg 76-78, B 1000 BRUXELLES 1.
☎ 13.37.36/12.05.60

BRAZIL – BRESIL
Mestre Jou S.A., Rua Guaipá 518,
Caixa Postal 24090, 05089 SAO PAULO 10.
☎ 256-2746/262-1609
Rua Senador Dantas 19 s/205-6, RIO DE
JANEIRO GB. ☎ 232-07. 32

CANADA
Information Canada
171 Slater, OTTAWA. KIA 0S9.
☎ (613) 992-9738

DENMARK – DANEMARK
Munksgaards Boghandel
Nørregade 6, 1165 KØBENHAVN K.
☎ (01) 12 69 70

FINLAND – FINLANDE
Akateeminen Kirjakauppa
Keskuskatu 1, 00100 HELSINKI 10. ☎ 625.901

FRANCE
Bureau des Publications de l'OCDE
2 rue André-Pascal, 75775 PARIS CEDEX 16.
☎ 524.81.67
Principaux correspondants :
13602 AIX-EN-PROVENCE : Librairie de
l'Université. ☎ 26.18.08
38000 GRENOBLE : B. Arthaud. ☎ 87.25.11
31000 TOULOUSE : Privat. ☎ 21.09.26

GERMANY – ALLEMAGNE
Verlag Weltarchiv G:m.b.H.
D 2000 HAMBURG 36, Neuer Jungfernstieg 21
☎ 040-35-62-501

GREECE – GRECE
Librairie Kauffmann, 28 rue du Stade,
ATHENES 132. ☎ 322.21.60

ICELAND – ISLANDE
Snaebjörn Jónsson and Co., h.f.,
Hafnarstræti 4 and 9, P.O.B. 1131,
REYKJAVIK. ☎ 13133/14281/11936

INDIA – INDE
Oxford Book and Stationery Co. :
NEW DELHI, Scindia House. ☎ 47388
CALCUTTA, 17 Park Street. ☎ 24083

IRELAND – IRLANDE
Eason and Son, 40 Lower O'Connell Street,
P.O.B. 42, DUBLIN 1. ☎ 01-41161

ISRAEL
Emanuel Brown :
35 Allenby Road, TEL AVIV. ☎ 51049/54082
also at :
9, Shlomzion Hamalka Street, JERUSALEM.
☎ 234807
48 Nahlath Benjamin Street, TEL AVIV.
☎ 53276

ITALY – ITALIE
Libreria Commissionaria Sansoni :
Via Lamarmora 45, 50121 FIRENZE. ☎ 579751
Via Bartolini 29, 20155 MILANO. ☎ 365083
Sous-dépositaires:
Editrice e Libreria Herder,
Piazza Montecitorio 120, 00186 ROMA.
☎ 674628
Libreria Hoepli, Via Hoepli 5, 20121 MILANO.
☎ 865446
Libreria Lattes, Via Garibaldi 3, 10122 TORINO.
☎ 519274
La diffusione delle edizioni OCDE è inoltre assicu-
rata dalle migliori librerie nelle città più importanti.

JAPAN – JAPON
OECD Publications Centre,
Akasaka Park Building,
2-3-4 Akasaka,
Minato-ku
TOKYO 107. ☎ 586-2016
Maruzen Company Ltd.,
6 Tori-Nichome Nihonbashi, TOKYO 103,
P.O.B. 5050, Tokyo International 100-31.
☎ 272-7211

LEBANON – LIBAN
Documenta Scientifica/Redico
Edison Building, Bliss Street,
P.O.Box 5641, BEIRUT. ☎ 354429 – 344425

THE NETHERLANDS – PAYS-BAS
W.P. Van Stockum
Buitenhof 36, DEN HAAG. ☎ 070-65.68.08

NEW ZEALAND – NOUVELLE-ZELANDE
The Publications Officer
Government Printing Office
Mulgrave Street (Private Bag)
WELLINGTON, ☎ 46.807
and Government Bookshops at
AUCKLAND (P.O.B. 5344). ☎ 32.919
CHRISTCHURCH (P.O.B. 1721). ☎ 50.331
HAMILTON (P.O.B. 857). ☎ 80.103
DUNEDIN (P.O.B. 1104). ☎ 78.294

NORWAY – NORVEGE
Johan Grundt Tanums Bokhandel,
Karl Johansgate 41/43, OSLO 1. ☎ 02-332980

PAKISTAN
Mirza Book Agency, 65 Shahrah Quaid-E-Azam,
LAHORE 3. ☎ 66839

PHILIPPINES
R.M. Garcia Publishing House,
903 Quezon Blvd. Ext., QUEZON CITY,
P.O. Box 1860 – MANILA. ☎ 99.98.47

PORTUGAL
Livraria Portugal,
Rua do Carmo 70-74. LISBOA 2. ☎ 360582/3

SPAIN – ESPAGNE
Libreria Mundi Prensa
Castelló 37, MADRID-1. ☎ 275.46.55
Libreria Bastinos
Pelayo, 52, BARCELONA 1. ☎ 222.06.00

SWEDEN – SUEDE
Fritzes Kungl. Hovbokhandel,
Fredsgatan 2, 11152 STOCKHOLM 16.
☎ 08/23 89 00

SWITZERLAND – SUISSE
Librairie Payot, 6 rue Grenus, 1211 GENEVE 11.
☎ 022-31.89.50

TAIWAN
Books and Scientific Supplies Services, Ltd.
P.O.B. 83, TAIPEI.

TURKEY – TURQUIE
Librairie Hachette,
469 Istiklal Caddesi,
Beyoglu, ISTANBUL, ☎ 44.94.70
et 14 E Ziya Gökalp Caddesi
ANKARA. ☎ 12.10.80

UNITED KINGDOM – ROYAUME-UNI
H.M. Stationery Office, P.O.B. 569, LONDON
SE1 9 NH, ☎ 01-928-6977, Ext. 410
or
49 High Holborn
LONDON WC1V 6HB (personal callers)
Branches at: EDINBURGH, BIRMINGHAM,
BRISTOL, MANCHESTER, CARDIFF,
BELFAST.

UNITED STATES OF AMERICA
OECD Publications Center, Suite 1207,
1750 Pennsylvania Ave, N.W.
WASHINGTON, D.C. 20006. ☎ (202)298-8755

VENEZUELA
Libreria del Este, Avda. F. Miranda 52,
Edificio Galipán, Aptdo. 60 337, CARACAS 106.
☎ 32 23 01/33 26 04/33 24 73

YUGOSLAVIA – YOUGOSLAVIE
Jugoslovenska Knjiga, Terazije 27, P.O.B. 36,
BEOGRAD. ☎ 621-992

Les commandes provenant de pays où l'OCDE n'a pas encore désigné de dépositaire
peuvent être adressées à :
OCDE, Bureau des Publications, 2 rue André-Pascal, 75775 Paris CEDEX 16
Orders and inquiries from countries where sales agents have not yet been appointed may be sent to
OECD, Publications Office, 2 rue André-Pascal, 75775 Paris CEDEX 16

OECD PUBLICATIONS
2, rue André-Pascal, 75775 Paris Cedex 16

No. 32801 - 1974
PRINTED IN FRANCE